S... Selling ONLINE

Guide

Linda
Parkinson-
Hardman

First published in Great Britain in 2013 by
Need2Know
Remus House
Coltsfoot Drive
Peterborough
PE2 9BF
Telephone 01733 898103
Fax 01733 313524
www.need2knowbooks.co.uk

Contents

Introduction

Do you have a house full of unwanted items cluttering up your cupboards and attic? Perhaps you are a crafter, a writer or a photographer who would like to make some extra income by selling your work online.

In the past you might have taken a stall at a car boot sale or approached a local gallery or shop to see if they would stock your work. However, with the huge advances and changes that have happened online in recent years, it has become much easier, quicker and cheaper to put what you want to sell in front of a much larger audience than ever before.

According to the Office for National Statistics, 85% of UK adults had used the Internet by autumn 2012, which is almost 43 million people. Many of these people are using the Internet to find information and buy the things you are planning to sell. The only requirement of you is to ensure that you can present your items to them at the right time for the right price.

However, this wealth of opportunity can also make it much harder to know where the best place to sell online is, as each opportunity will have its own rules and requirements. This can create indecision and some people will give up at the first hurdle. Yet, with a little knowledge and understanding about how the rules can affect you in particular, you will be able to make the right decisions from the outset and avoid wasting money displaying items that won't sell because they are in the wrong place.

Although this informative, easy-to-read book is written for the online seller who is just starting out, it has a wealth of hints and tips that can make a big difference to those who have been using the Internet to sell online for some time.

The aim of this book is to make sure your online selling activities are both profitable and enjoyable. Throughout, you will explore ideas about the sorts of things you could sell online, including some you probably haven't even thought of before.

You will also learn which of the various websites can help you sell your particular products and whether having your own website is a good idea. Also you will find out how to create a product listing with great descriptions and images that stand out from the crowd.

Of course, selling online needs to be profitable and you will learn how to price your products correctly so that they sell for the most amount of money.

Most online sellers will also want to encourage as many people as possible to pay for the things they buy immediately with a credit or debit card and there is information about simple systems such as PayPal and the more complex and expensive third party options such as WorldPay.

If you decide that having your own website is something you're considering then it's important that you understand all the choices and requirements that you'll need to consider. This includes introducing some quick and simple ways to set up shop in just a matter of hours.

Of course, marketing your products is essential and you'll find out how you can spread the word about the things you are selling through more focused marketing activities.

A book about online selling wouldn't be complete without a more in-depth look at how Amazon and eBay can be used by new and experienced sellers. Finally we must remember that there are also tax and legal obligations to take account of too.

Throughout, you will find simple tasks to follow and clear instructions about how to use the various websites and pieces of software. In the appendices you will find sets of resources to help you calculate costs, lists of useful websites and helpful companies, an explanation of some of the jargon used and a list of reference material referred to.

Please note, words or terms that appear in italics can be found in the glossary towards the end of the book.

Acknowledgements

I would like to thank Anna and Amy at Need2Know for being on the end of my questions and queries. And I'd like to send a huge hug to the lovely Stevie for letting me off normal business duties so that I could write this book and also for reading through many drafts and listening to many quotes.

Disclaimer

The material in this guide is set out in good faith and is intended for general information and guidance and no liability can be accepted for loss or expense incurred as a result of relying on particular circumstances on a statement made in this guide.

The laws and regulations around selling online are complex and liable to change without notice and readers should check the current position with the relevant authorities. It is not intended to replace any professional business or financial advice that you may also receive.

All the information in this book was correct at the time of going to press. It is important to remember that third party websites can change their terms and conditions without reference to their users at any time and therefore it is very important that you read any messages you are sent about such changes in a timely fashion.

All costs quoted in this book are those listed by individual services at the time of writing. Costs shown in other currencies have been converted to pounds sterling using the website www.xe.com for current exchange rates. Be aware that exchange rates fluctuate and the actual cost you pay may be considerably different to what is quoted in this book.

Chapter One

Getting Started

In the beginning

Selling online has come a long way since the early years of the Web when all you could do was provide would-be customers with a form to print off which they would send to you with a cheque. Over the years this situation has changed dramatically; initially it was only the largest of organisations who could afford to process credit and debit card payments online through *merchant services*, as such systems often cost hundreds of thousands of pounds to implement and then thousands of pounds each month to run.

By the early part of this century, with the continued development of auction websites like eBay, it became apparent that a simple, online payment processing system was needed that allowed everyone to participate, regardless of who they were. In March 2000, eBay acquired PayPal specifically to allow its sellers to take payments securely online. Since then, a whole host of online payment processing options have become available to even the smallest of sellers. This means that taking payments, even as small as £1, has become economically viable for everyone. As a result, anyone, no matter who they are or where they live, can use the Internet to successfully sell their unwanted and other items online simply and easily.

Definition of online selling

Online selling is a form of electronic commerce or *ecommerce*, which allows consumers and purchasers to buy goods or services directly from the person selling them over the Internet.

Online selling can happen in two different places, through the seller's own website or via a third party website that allows them to list their product or service, in exchange for a fee. The largest of the online retailing sites are eBay and Amazon and items for sale on these sites by online sellers are usually called *Listings*.

Who can sell online?

Almost anyone can sell online as long as they meet any minimum age restrictions. The age restriction is typically 18 years of age. This is because in most cases you will need to provide a personal credit or debit card for the payment of fees. This applies both to sites such as eBay and Amazon as well as your own website, especially if you are planning to use services like PayPal to process payments.

Five step online sales process

The process of selling online has not changed despite all the advances in technology. The only things that are different are the means and activities that surround online selling which have become much easier to understand and cheaper to access.

There are five important steps to completing a successful sale online and we will be covering each of these in different chapters within this book.

The process that someone goes through in order to sell something online is:

1. Finding something to sell.

2. Listing the product in the right place for the right buyer to find at the right time.

3. Attracting potential customers to the product listing and encouraging them to add it to their shopping basket.

4. Completing the payment process.

5. Sending the goods to the customer.

'Online selling can happen in two different places, through the seller's own website or via a third party website that allows them to list their product or service, in exchange for a fee.'

Each step is equally important in the process and each must take place in order for the sale to complete satisfactorily. However, there are lots of things to think about as a customer moves from one step to the next.

You need to think about things like where your products are coming from, where are you going to sell them, how customers will find and pay for them and finally, how you will deliver the products (or indeed services) to them.

This book is designed to walk you through each of these steps, helping you to explore all the options by making suggestions and offering alternatives, so that by the end you are confident you can make your online selling activities as simple and easy as possible.

Before we get started though, we need to look at few of the basic considerations, such as why you want to sell online, what you might be selling and what skills and equipment you might need.

Why sell online?

The reasons people sell things online vary from the occasional de-clutterer who wants to make a few pounds instead of sending everything to the local charity shop, to the online entrepreneur who is hoping to replace their full-time income. Of course, there are many variations to this simplified model, but understanding what you want to achieve at the outset will help you enormously when it comes to deciding where to focus your efforts and your products. Invariably, some things you can do online are easier than others.

You will also need to take into account the amount of time you have available for your online endeavours. If you work full-time and have a family then you will probably have little time each week to spend on your online selling activities. If, however, you are single or have just been made redundant, for example, then you may want to spend as much time as is available to you, building up a solid main or second income. Neither of these options is more right than the other, they simply suit different situations.

Of course it is worth remembering that things change and your decision to start selling online may be fuelled by one necessity but end up being driven by something else entirely. The beauty of selling online is that this sort of change can be very quick and easy to accomplish.

'Understanding what you want to achieve at the outset will help you enormously when it comes to deciding where to focus your efforts and your products.'

What will you sell online?

The most obvious and easiest way to start selling online is simply to clear your house of those unwanted items that have been lying around taking up valuable space. They might include unwanted Christmas and birthday gifts, toys that your children have grown out of but which are still in good condition, books you no longer read, CDs and records you no longer listen to or even items from the attic you suspect may have a value beyond the obvious. Each of these items could be just what someone else is looking for, someone who will value and treasure it more than you do.

Of course, you could also pack everything up and take it to a local car boot sale, but that often involves early mornings, standing around in cold and wet weather and an assumption that the right buyer will pass your stall.

'According to eBay, there are 14 million active members in the UK, over 40% of regular Internet users visit eBay every month.'

According to eBay, there are 14 million active members in the UK, over 40% of regular Internet users visit eBay every month. (Source: eBay Company Overview. Source: eBay.co.uk, accessed 20 February 2013). Statistics such as this might persuade an unwilling car-booter to try something different instead.

Crafters

Perhaps you are a crafter making anything from hand-knitted socks to jewellery and greeting cards. There are many specialist websites now catering to this large online community.

Etsy is the largest online shopping cart for crafters and has over 22 million members operating in 200 different countries and makes it easy for anyone to find something completely unique to give as a gift to a relative or friend. (Etsy Statistics. Source: Etsy Press Page, accessed 20 February 2013)

See the following chapter for more information on Etsy.

Authors and writers

You might be a budding author who has a book or a number of short stories you would like to sell. The rise of the Amazon Kindle has seen an explosion of independent, self-publishing authors making an impact on many readers' lives.

In August 2012, four self-published authors could be found in the New York Times Bestseller lists including Colleen Hoover, RL Matthewson, Bella Andre and EL James, author of the *50 Shades of Grey* trilogy (Source: The Guardian 22nd February 2013). In the UK the most successful self-published author is Kerry Wilkinson, the author of *Locked In*. (Source: The Guardian 21st February 2013).

Even if you don't make it to the bestseller lists though, it is possible to make a substantial extra income by selling your books and stories online. You can sell them in digital formats and in paperback and hardback formats through *print on demand* services such as Lulu (see chapter 2).

Photographers and digital artists

Photographers and digital artists can also attract a share of the online selling phenomenon through sites such as Dreamstime and Shutterstock (see the next chapter). These sites sell *royalty free* stock photography to those who need images to illustrate things like websites, brochures, magazine articles and book covers.

The term 'royalty free' does not mean that the image is free of charge; it means that once the fee has been paid, the purchaser has the right to use it within certain restrictions.

Fine artists

Fine artists are catered for through sites such as Etsy, as well as many other specialist online art retailers who will take a small commission in return for exhibiting your work in an online gallery. In some cases, they will allow you to create items such as posters and prints that you can also sell.

Musicians

Musicians can share their music and songs with the world through sites such as CD Baby and CreateSpace (see page 23). Using sites such as these means that distributing CDs and digital downloads on sites like Amazon and the iStore became so much easier.

Skills and services

Even those who don't believe they have any creative skills at all can sell their services and skills online.

People will book all sorts of things from dog walking to typing through the Internet and sites like Freelancer UK and Elance allow you to bid on jobs that are posted by businesses seeking help. Fiverr allows you to tell people what you will do in exchange for small amounts of money and items on offer can range from answering philosophy questions to researching family trees. Go to page 24 for more information on the sites mentioned here.

Are there any restrictions on what I can sell online?

'Even those who don't believe they have any creative skills at all can sell their services and skills online.'

With the exception of illegal or restricted items that may need a licence, there are very few restrictions on what can be sold online through your own website. However, if you want to sell through sites like eBay then you will need to be aware of their terms and conditions.

Typically, the things you can't sell or which may be restricted include live animals, firearms, adult-only items, weapons of any description, animal products, drugs (illegal and legal), hazardous materials such as chemicals, human remains and body parts, offensive materials, foods and healthcare items and items which might encourage illegal activities.

On other sites, such as Amazon Marketplace or CafePress, you may be restricted to the items that they already have listed in their inventory.

What skills will I need to sell online?

There are a few core skills you will need that will help you sell online effectively, regardless of the products you have and why you are selling them. The most important skill is probably the ability to describe your products and services accurately and with enough difference that they stand out from the mass you will be competing with. This requires reasonably good skills in English.

The second skill you will need is the ability to take a good, clear image of any physical products from a variety of different angles. You will also need to be able to make calculations to help you when it comes to pricing your products and services so you make a profit. We will be looking at all of these in chapter 3 of this book.

What equipment do I need to sell online?

The basic equipment needed includes a computer with a reasonably fast broadband connection. You will also require a private email account where you can receive messages from your customers and notifications about products you have sold. This should not be an email account given to you by your employer and you might want to investigate using a Hotmail or Gmail account.

A reasonable camera will allow you to take photographs of any products you wish to sell. Although many mobile phones have pretty good cameras built into them and their photographs are probably acceptable for low-value items, they are unlikely to produce the quality of image required for high-value items.

You will also need a printer for any invoices and packing slips you need to include with your sold items.

Finally, you will need packing materials such as padded envelopes, bubble wrap, brown paper and strong tape. You should include a return address label on the back of every order sent out just in case it isn't delivered.

In addition, and depending on what you are selling, you might want to invest in some specialist software such as Photoshop which will allow you to manipulate images easily; although I will explain how to resize an image with the free utility Paint which is included with every Windows computer in chapter 3.

'You can get started with just a computer, camera, printer, packing materials and a private email account.'

Summing Up

- Selling online has been made much easier for everyone to do. Services are now available that allow you to take payments online simply and quickly.

- Anyone can sell online as long as they are over the age of 18.

- You may want to sell online because you want to make some money instead of sending clutter to the charity shop or because you want to supplement your income on a permanent basis.

- There are five clear steps to completing a successful sale online, these include choosing a product, creating a listing, attracting customers, making a payment and posting the product to a buyer.

- You can sell many things online including unwanted items, books you have written, music you have created, photographs you have taken and even skills or services.

- Some things can't be sold online because they are illegal or require a licence and you will need to be aware of what they are when you come to list your items.

- You will need to be able to write in clear English, take photographs and do simple maths to help you list products successfully and price them correctly.

- You can sell online successfully with only a computer, printer, camera, email account and packing materials.

Chapter Two

Where to Sell Online

Most people new to online selling assume that eBay is the only site to use. It is true that eBay is one of the largest online market places in the world. It was launched in the UK in 1999 and is used by 14 million people. They claim that 10 million items are listed on the UK site at any one time (eBay Company Overview. Source: eBay.co.uk accessed 20th May 2013).

It's not surprising that this is the often the first port of call. However, there are many alternatives to eBay and some may be more appropriate than others for your items.

How do I choose where to sell?

Before we talk about individual sites there are some questions you need to ask yourself:

* What am I selling?

* Why am I selling it?

* Do I need to be available 24/7?

* How will people find it?

* What will it cost me to sell it?

What you are selling will dictate where you sell. For example if you are selling something physical such as a dress, crockery or a toy then you will probably use an auction site. Alternatively, if it's an e-book then you will need a specialist site that caters for this type of product.

Understanding which site works best with which type of product is crucial to deciding the right site for your items.

'Understanding which site works best with which type of product is crucial to deciding the right site for your items.'

If you are clearing clutter or simply getting rid of unwanted Christmas gifts then you probably don't need a fully functional online shop. Instead, somewhere you can list items on an occasional basis will be the perfect solution. However, if you are planning to create regular extra income by sourcing and selling stock then a different approach may be necessary.

Some sites selling digital items or services deal with the whole process from start to finish on your behalf, simply paying you your earnings each month. Others require you to monitor activity, take payment and then ship the goods out to the customer.

Wherever you list your product you will need to be sure that customers can find it. On some sites the description will be written for you, on others you will need to choose the category, add the keywords and create a description yourself.

'Online marketplaces are ideal for occasional sales. It is easy to set up an account and items are listed within minutes.'

It is rare to be able to sell something completely free of charge. Even with your own website there will be fees to pay. Most sites you list items on will take a small commission based on the cost you set for your item. You need to be sure what the costs are as it's this that will determine whether you make a profit or lose money instead.

Online marketplaces

Online marketplaces are ideal for occasional sales. It is easy to set up an account and items are listed within minutes. They tend to operate on trust and this is achieved by allowing buyers to comment on the purchase process and leave feedback.

The biggest online marketplaces in the UK are undoubtedly Amazon and eBay and they are both described in more detail in chapters 8 and 9. Other online marketplaces include Play, Etsy, Alibris and Gumtree.

These sites require you to respond to requests for information about the items you list and then send the items to the buyer.

Some sites allow you to find your product in their catalogue and simply mark your price against it; others require you to write a detailed description.

Play

Play is the UK's third largest online marketplace. Sellers can offer CDs, DVDs, books, games and more through its sister site PlayTrade and are charged 10% of the value of the item plus 50p per item sold.

There is a 5% charge to withdraw your balance to a bank account but if you buy something from Play.com with your funds instead there is no withdrawal fee.

For example if you sell a DVD for £15 you receive £13 (£15 − £1.50 (10% charge) − 50p = £13). You are charged 65p (5% of £13) to withdraw your money to a bank account. This means you will receive £12.35 in your bank account.

PlayTrade hold funds for 21 days before allowing transfer to a bank account or release it for spending on their website.

Etsy

Etsy is a large community of 22 million people set up in 2005 for crafters selling handmade items, craft supplies and vintage goods (items over 20 years old). They charge $0.20 (about 10p) to list an item for four months and then 3.5% of the sale price when it is sold.

All payments are made into a seller's own PayPal account or by cheque.

Alibris

Alibris is a specialist marketplace that has been selling books, music and films since 1998. Having an account on Alibris allows users to sell on all the major media sites including Amazon in the UK and Barnes and Noble in the US.

Their fees for the basic seller account include an annual fee of $19.99 (about £12) and $1 (about 65p) for every item sold.

Funds over a certain level are paid directly to a bank account.

Gumtree

Gumtree is the UK's number one classified ads site and is owned by eBay. It is the closest thing we have to the classified ads section of the local paper.

It also provides listings of jobs, flats and houses to rent or buy, services to the community such as plumbers and electricians and even pets.

It is free of charge to put an advert on Gumtree in most categories. The exceptions are home rentals, jobs and services.

Free adverts can be given more exposure by making them featured at a cost of £4.99. Adverts can also appear further up the listings through *bumping up* by payment of a small amount depending on the category.

'The biggest difference between a marketplace and auction website is that in a marketplace the price of the goods you sell are fixed.'

Auction websites

The biggest difference between a marketplace and auction website is that in a marketplace the price of the goods you sell are fixed. You set the price and that's what the buyer pays.

In an auction the price is fluid. You might set a starting price but where it ends up depends on how much someone wants that particular item.

Although the basic fees on auction sites are fixed it is easy for large bills to mount up when you add extras to help make your listing stand out. For instance, you will probably incur fees if you want to add extra photographs.

A basic listing on an auction site allows you to create a title for your listing, add it to a category, give it a description, add a photograph and choose some keywords. All auction sites require you to respond to requests for information about the items you list and then send the items to the buyer.

The biggest auction website is eBay and you will find a more detailed explanation about how it can be used in chapter 9.

Other auction websites include eBid and CQOut and Specialist Auctions.

eBid

eBid started just before eBay, in 1999. An independent survey noted that the two services were very similar in their user ratings (Top Ten Alternatives To eBay. Source: Online Auction Sites accessed 20/03/13). However the fees for eBid are significantly lower as items are listed free of charge with a *final valuation fee* of just 3.75% when sold.

Payments can be processed with PayPal, Google Wallet or Moneybookers. Each of these payment processing options is discussed in more detail in chapter 5.

CQout

CQout (pronounced 'seek you out') is very similar to eBid but with a much smaller audience. They charge a *user verification fee* of £2 by charging the credit or debit card you use to sign up to the service to validate your details.

Basic listings are free of charge and the final valuation fee is between 5.4%, if the item is below £50 and 3.6% if it is over £1000.

Rather than processing fees through PayPal, CQout uses SecurePay and it is the buyer that pays the *payment processing* charge. Sellers do not need an account with SecurePay themselves.

Payments are transferred to a bank account free of charge at the end of each month although they can be paid earlier for a small fee.

SpecialistAuctions.com

SpecialistAuctions.com sells rare, vintage and collectible items across several dozen categories ranging from clothes to police collectibles.

It is free to register with the site although they do limit new members to a £20 credit limit until they prove themselves.

There are no listing fees and the final valuation fee is just 3% of the amount an item sells for. Users can pay an additional 50p to make a listing bold or £1 to highlight it.

Buyers can pay by cheque, PayPal or Google Wallet directly to a bank account.

Selling digital products

So far in this chapter we have focused on selling physical items, things you can touch and feel and that you will almost certainly need to post to the buyer. It is possible that most of these items will be gathered from clearing out attics, wardrobes or bookshelves.

But what if you are a photographer, a musician or a writer, are there any services where you can sell your creative wares?

Broadly, the services that sell this type of product fall into two main categories, third party sites and on-demand services.

Third party websites allow you to list a digital product (photograph, e-book, music file or video). Every time it is bought it is delivered automatically to the buyer's computer or email account without any further intervention by you. Examples of such websites include Dreamstime and the Amazon Kindle store.

On-demand services work in a similar way to third party sites but for physical products instead. You add a file containing your music track, formatted book or video to the service. When someone buys the item, the CD, book or DVD is manufactured and posted out on your behalf. Examples of such services are CD Baby, Lulu and Createspace.

In both instances you set the price for your item and the service website charges a small commission for manufacturing and postage. The difference between the price you set and the commission charged is your *royalty payment* and is what you receive in your bank account.

You can find more information about Createspace and Amazon Kindle in chapter 8.

Dreamstime

Dreamstime is one of many online sites that allow photographers and digital artists to sell their work. Such sites allow people to search for and buy *royalty free* images. This means the buyer has the right to use that image for the purposes outlined in the agreement document.

Typically, an image on Dreamstime could be used as a cover for a book, on a T-shirt, in a magazine or on a greeting card. There are limits to how many times it may be used on an individual item but these limits extend into the thousands.

Image creators receive a revenue share of between 25% and 50% of the amount each image is sold for and can request payment into their bank account whenever the balance is greater than $100 (about £66).

CD Baby

CD Baby specialises in music and audio compositions. It's the perfect place for musicians and bands to sell directly to fans. However it also enables the sale of both physical CDs and downloads through online sites such as Amazon, iTunes and Google Play.

Musicians set their own prices and CD Baby charges $4 (about £3) commission. They also make an initial charge to set up each single or album added to CD Baby. At present the costs are $12.95 and $49 respectively (about £9 and £35).

CD Baby takes care of the CD production, packing and shipping and the artist takes a royalty payment. The royalty payment is the difference between the price set by the musician and the $4 commission charge.

Lulu

Lulu is the author's equivalent of CD Baby. It allows authors to create physical books, e-books, photo books and calendars.

When a hardback or paperback book is ordered it is printed, packed and shipped directly to the purchaser.

'CD Baby specialises in music and audio compositions. It's the perfect place for musicians and bands to sell directly to fans.'

Authors can also add their books to global distribution networks allowing them to be sold on Amazon, in WH Smith and even Tesco Online.

It is free to create a book although there is a charge to add it to the global book sale distribution channels. Authors set their own prices and receive the difference between the price they set and the cost of production as a *royalty payment*.

Selling services and skills online

The final section of this chapter is for those readers who would like to sell services online. Perhaps you are a champion dog-walker, bookkeeper, proofreader or typist. Whatever service you offer you can sell it online through sites like Freelancer, Elance, Fiverr or even Craigslist.

Elance and Freelancer UK

Both of these sites work in very similar ways and cater for those who need services and those who provide services.

The majority of the work found through these sites falls into one of the following categories: IT and programming, design and multimedia, writing and translation, sales and marketing, admin support, engineering and manufacturing, finance and management or legal.

Both sites take a small percentage of the quote agreed between buyer and seller as their fee. This is paid when the work is completed to the buyer's satisfaction.

Elance currently charge a service fee of 8.75% and Freelancer charge £3.50 or 10% of the cost of the project whichever is greater.

Fiverr

Fiverr gives everyone a chance to sell their services and expertise regardless of what that is. Everything from Italian lessons via the Internet to discussions about philosophy can be bought and sold and each offer starts at just $5 (about £3.50).

The categories for services include gifts, graphics and design, video and animation, online marketing, writing and translation, advertising, business, programming and technical, music and audio, fun and bizarre and lifestyle.

If you wanted to offer a service like cleaning or dog-walking you would add it to the lifestyle category.

Fiverr charge 20% for every $5 you earn which means you only receive $4 (about £2.60).

Craigslist

Craigslist is a global noticeboard catering for local communities. It allows you to list items for sale or services you offer in much the same way you might use a newspaper classified ads section.

Most users of Craigslist will never be charged for the items or services they offer through the site. Craigslist makes its money by charging those who are offering jobs and some types of accommodation.

The biggest limitation of Craigslist is that only 27 areas are actually listed for the UK although some of these are for counties rather than cities.

Summing Up

- There are many different places that you can sell online. Each caters for different types of seller and product.

- The difference between an auction site and a marketplace is that the price of items in a marketplace is fixed by the seller. In an auction the prices are more fluid and dependent on who is bidding.

- Specialist online marketplaces such as Etsy and Alibris allow you to sell specific items such as handmade crafts and books.

- You can sell digital products like photographs or music through sites such as Dreamstime and CD Baby.

- Babysitters or dog walkers can offer their services online on fiverr.com, Craigslist or even Gumtree.

- If you have specialist skills such as writing or computing you can offer yourself to businesses that need these services through freelancer.co.uk or elance.com

- Royalty payments are made to the creators of music, videos, photographs and books. This is the difference between the price charged to the buyer and cost of manufacture and shipping.

- In almost all cases there will be charges involved in selling online ranging from listing fees to final sale valuations and charges to withdraw money to bank accounts.

- Some sites charge to add extra information or additional photographs to listings.

set they will need to make sure the final price, which needs to inc[...] costs, is roughly the same. Too high means purchasers won't buy a[...] choose other sellers, yet too low means that sellers don't make as mu[...]

Pricing handmade or rare products

Handmade or rare items need a little more research before deciding on the right price. A good starting point is knowledge of what comparable items sell for on your chosen marketplace.

For example, if I were selling handmade cards I would probably do a search on Etsy for similar greetings cards. This allows me to find out who my competitors are and what an average price is.

'Being aware of what other people charge is just one thing you need to know when pricing a product.'.

Being aware of what other people charge is just one thing you need to know when pricing a product. Other important things that need to be taken into account include how much you charge for the time you take to make each item (especially if they are made to order) plus the cost of any materials you have used. This is your *cost price*.

The calculation looks like this:

materials + time = basic price

example: £1 + £5 = £6

Your cost price is the minimum amount you should sell your item for.

Other costs you need to take into account include the fees to list an item on your chosen site, any payment processing fees and postage costs.

You may also have additional costs in the form of *overheads*. These are costs you have to pay regardless of whether you sell anything or not and could include things like printer paper, ink and even electricity. Some overheads will be fixed such as monthly subscription fees; others might be a *variable overhead cost* which are dependent on how much you use something

Calculating the cost of overheads can be quite daunting but a simple way to do it might be to take the overhead cost, say of a printer ink cartridge, and divide it by the number of items you make in the length of time you use it for. This is fairly arbitrary but it does mean that you will have a consistent amount [...] add on to each price.

Chapter Three

Pricing and Promoting Your Products

Deciding on the right price for something depends on some things you can control and others you can't.

Your product prices will also be affected by why you are selling. If you are simply selling unwanted items you probably won't worry if you meet the original cost or not. If you are selling to supplement your income though you will need to be sure that you aren't making a loss because you don't have the right pricing strategy.

The difference between what it costs to create, make or buy your product and the price you sell it for is known as your *gross profit*.

'Deciding on the right price for something depends som

Pricing fixed price products

Fixed price items are those which are readily available and inclu clothes, electronic items and other mass-produced goods.

The advantage of a selling a product like this is that y decision about what to charge as the manufactur done that for you already. The disadvantage a healthy profit if everyone is selling the same

For example, a search of Amazon reveals that a a recommended retail price of £16.99 which has be £9.75 (accessed 21st April 2013). If anyone is selling

28

Chapter Three

Pricing and Promoting Your Products

Deciding on the right price for something depends on some things you can control and others you can't.

Your product prices will also be affected by why you are selling. If you are simply selling unwanted items you probably won't worry if you meet the original cost or not. If you are selling to supplement your income though you will need to be sure that you aren't making a loss because you don't have the right pricing strategy.

The difference between what it costs to create, make or buy your product and the price you sell it for is known as your *gross profit*.

Pricing fixed price products

Fixed price items are those which are readily available and include books, clothes, electronic items and other mass-produced goods.

The advantage of a selling a product like this is that you don't have to make a decision about what to charge as the manufacturer and other sellers have done that for you already. The disadvantage is you have little scope for making a healthy profit if everyone is selling the same product at the same price.

For example, a search of Amazon reveals that a brand new Monopoly set has a recommended retail price of £16.99 which has been been discounted to £9.75 (accessed 21st April 2013). If anyone is selling a new or second-hand

'Deciding on the right price for something depends on some things you can control and others you can't.'

set they will need to make sure the final price, which needs to include postage costs, is roughly the same. Too high means purchasers won't buy as they can choose other sellers, yet too low means that sellers don't make as much profit.

Pricing handmade or rare products

Handmade or rare items need a little more research before deciding on the right price. A good starting point is knowledge of what comparable items sell for on your chosen marketplace.

For example, if I were selling handmade cards I would probably do a search on Etsy for similar greetings cards. This allows me to find out who my competitors are and what an average price is.

'Being aware of what other people charge is just one thing you need to know when pricing a product.'.

Being aware of what other people charge is just one thing you need to know when pricing a product. Other important things that need to be taken into account include how much you charge for the time you take to make each item (especially if they are made to order) plus the cost of any materials you have used. This is your *cost price*.

The calculation looks like this:

materials + time = basic price

example: £1 + £5 = £6

Your cost price is the minimum amount you should sell your item for.

Other costs you need to take into account include the fees to list an item on your chosen site, any payment processing fees and postage costs.

You may also have additional costs in the form of *overheads*. These are costs you have to pay regardless of whether you sell anything or not and could include things like printer paper, ink and even electricity. Some overheads will be fixed such as monthly subscription fees; others might be a *variable overhead cost* which are dependent on how much you use something

Calculating the cost of overheads can be quite daunting but a simple way to do it might be to take the overhead cost, say of a printer ink cartridge, and divide it by the number of items you make in the length of time you use it for. This is fairly arbitrary but it does mean that you will have a consistent amount to add on to each price.

The calculation looks like this:

cost of overhead item ÷ number of items made = overhead cost

example: £10 ÷ 100 = 10p

Working out these costs in advance means you can be clear about what you need to charge for everything you sell.

It's also to important to know these figures because if you are able to sell on more than one website then the deciding factor might be the charges each site adds to your costs. Using a site which costs more to use than another would mean that you have a smaller profit. However, if that site is likely to sell more items then it may be worth accepting a smaller profit.

The calculation to take into account website fees may look more like this:

cost price + overhead costs + website fees + shipping = basic price

example: £6 + £0.10 + £2.20 + £1.10 = £9.40

When you have a basic price you can decide on your *profit margin*. You may set your profit margin at 10% which adds a further 94p to the above figure making your selling price £10.34.

How does the figure you come up with for your item compare with your competitors and their products? If they are charging less then you will need to revise your plan. Perhaps you can use cheaper materials or work more quickly when you have more skill. You might need to change how you post the item or the percentage you add as profit.

Your items need to be as close to what other people charge as possible because otherwise they won't sell. If they are charging more then you can either increase your profit margin or keep the price you have set and see if you sell more items.

You will find a set of forms in Appendix 1, Calculation sheets, that can help you work out your costs.

Pricing digital products

For some people the time to make or create the item is less important to their *selling price* than for crafts or mass-produced products. This is because they may be creating digital goods like photographs, music tracks or e-books. The nature of these products is that they can be sold many times over to lots of different buyers on many different websites.

For example, the same digital photograph can appear on Dreamstime, Shutterstock, Fotolia and iStockPhoto. Which website a photographer chooses to use might be decided solely by the fees they charge.

Such sellers may choose to ignore the time it takes to create the original item and set a price based solely on what their competitors charge for similar items. There is, however, one set of costs they must take into account and that will be the cost of equipment they might need to create their digital products such as computers, cameras or specialist software. They may also pay monthly account or listing fees.

Digital producers can account for the cost of equipment by using a variation of the overhead cost. The total cost of equipment is usually accounted for over a period of three or four years. This means that the cost of equipment is divided by three or four and one third or quarter is set against the cost of making products each year.

If I buy a computer costing £300 and account for it over three years, this means that each year I am telling myself that it has cost me an additional £100 to produce my products and I must take this into account when I am setting my prices.

If I then create and sell 50 items I can divide the year's cost by 50 and work out that the cost of creating each one must include an extra £2 in my final selling price.

The calculation looks like this:

equipment cost $\div$ 3 $\div$ number of items produced = equipment overhead

example: £300 $\div$ 3 $\div$ 50 = £2

Promoting your products

In some cases the promotion is done for you when you list an item. For example adding a book to Amazon means it appears against the main listing as an additional copy for sale. There is little that can be done to highlight a specific book other than by making it the cheapest available. We will be exploring more about Amazon in chapter 8.

In most cases though, you will need to create your own set of details which includes photographs, descriptions, categories and keywords.

Getting the details right

Many product listings on eBay fail because their creators forget one simple rule; they forget to add any specific details for their item when they list it. Specific details include things like the *ISBN number* if it's a book or the product number and version if it's electrical, brand names, product names, version numbers, the year or date it was created or published, a publisher's name and author details.

Many buyers search for specific items by typing in the version they are looking for. If I were looking to buy my printer I might type in 'Canon MP220 Printer'. Listings which have these details are more likely to show up on sites like eBay than those that just use the words 'Canon Printer'.

Photographing products

Other listings fail on the quality of the photographs. People will often add items that have no image or a poor photograph which barely shows the product at all.

A good image is created when you have a good light source behind you. The best light source is natural daylight and if you are photographing indoors then you should position yourself between the window and your item.

Ideally, you would put your item on a table laid with a white cloth. If your item is larger then try to position it against a neutral background such as a white or cream wall or plain tiles. Taking the time to do this means viewers get a clearer picture of what you are selling.

'Many product listings on eBay fail because their creators forget one simple rule; they forget to add any specific details for their item when they list it.'

Before pressing the shutter on your camera select the highest resolution of image that your camera (or phone) has and then centre the item in the viewfinder.

Take close-up photographs of any badges, maker's marks, signatures and brand names. You can also use a reference like a ruler placed next to the product if size is important.

Where there are problems or signs of wear and tear then it is important to photograph these and point them out in your description.

Try to think about what the buyer might be looking for when taking photographs. For example, a collector might prefer a few really good close-up photographs whilst a parent looking for a toy might just want to the see that the box is intact.

If the item you are selling has moving parts then the buyer might want to be reassured that it is in working order. You could record a short video of it working on a smart phone and upload it to YouTube.

'Try to think about what the buyer might be looking for when taking photographs.'

Editing and resizing an image in Paint

Most computers these days come with some sort of picture software included. On a PC this is called Paint and it can be found in the accessories folder on your start button.

Paint allows you to draw on a picture you have taken adding arrows to highlight any problem areas. You can also resize the picture files if you have taken photographs that are very large as some sites only allow small file sizes.

To resize an image in Paint, click on the Image tab and select Resize and Skew. Change the values on the horizontal and vertical boxes to 50% and click OK. This will reduce your file size by 50% and the size of the image by 50%. (Don't forget to save your picture before you close Paint down.)

Creating a great product description

A product description is the most important part of any listing. This is because most people will search sites using the keywords and phrases they think are relevant. When a description uses the words and phrases potential buyers also use, you give yourself a a greater chance of selling.

If you are new to creating keywords the important thing to remember is that they are words that your potential buyers are likely to use and as such they may be different from the words you might use to describe something.

One way to find out keywords is to use the Google Keyword Tool. This is a free online utility that allows you to see how many people are searching Google for specific terms and phrases. You can find it by searching for 'Google Keyword Tool' on your favourite search engine.

When you have loaded the keyword tool simply type in a word or short phrase and follow the onscreen instructions. The site will then display a list of up to 100 words and phrases with the details of how many people have searched for each globally and locally (in the UK) over the previous 30 days.

For example, I typed in the phrase 'Radley changing bag 'and saw that other searches include 'Radley baby bag' and 'yummy mummy changing bag'. This told me that these are phrases that I should also think about using when describing this particular product.

'When a description uses the words and phrases potential buyers also use, you give yourself a a greater chance of selling.'

Crafting the title of your listing

The starting point of a listing is the title. This may be fixed as in the titles of books you or others have written and which are being sold in the online bookshops. In most cases, though, you will be able to craft a title that contains specific words that are likely to be important to the buyer like the brand name, size, title, number or version, colour, condition, artist or designer.

An example of a good title for a designer handbag might be 'Brand New Radley Great British Summer Limited Edition Signature Bag 2011'. The reason this title works is because it tells the searcher exactly what they are going to see when they click on the link that takes them to the description. It includes the keywords 'Radley', 'Signature Bag', 'Great British Summer' and '2012'.

Writing a listing description

A description is your opportunity to give the buyer more information about the product you are selling. It should highlight all the important elements. It is important that the spelling and grammar are correct. Full sentences and proper punctuation are very important because a misplaced comma can affect the meaning of an entire paragraph or sentence.

Before you create your listing it is important to think about the following questions:

- Who is likely to want to buy my product?
- Why will they be using it?
- Is their experience likely to be important?

Having the answers to these questions will help you to frame your description appropriately.

For instance, let's say you are selling an older iPad. It is likely that the buyer is going to be someone trying one out for the first time as someone who has been using one for a while would be more likely to buy a newer version. Therefore your buyer's experience might be minimal.

Whilst they will need to know the basics they may not understand all the technical terminology that the iPad product specification gives. Explaining what it will do in layman's terms would be an advantage.

For example saying 'With Wi-Fi support and a 10-hour battery life this 16GB Apple iPad means you can stay connected to the world all the time' means more to the average reader than any technical jargon relating to storage and hardware capacity.

These questions work in almost all situations whether you are selling hand-crafted items or unwanted Christmas gifts.

The first paragraph is the most important and should include all the item specifics like size, shape (if it's important), manufacturer, brand name, when it was purchased, notable features and anything exceptional such as signatures or history. Repeating the keywords from your title in the first paragraph is also a good idea.

'A description is your opportunity to give the buyer more information about the product you are selling. It should highlight all the important elements.'

The condition of the item should be made quite clear to the buyer and if it is damaged or soiled then this needs to be both explained within the description and shown in photographs.

Ensure you include the details of exactly what is included in the offer; for example are you including batteries or cables? If anything is missing then this needs to be noted as well so that possible buyers can make a decision based on what they might have to add to the product in order to use it.

Depending on the website you are using you may need to include information about postage. In some cases you may decide that the item is to be collected from you especially if it is expensive, heavy or large.

Using keywords and tags

Some online selling sites allow you to create a set of keywords or tags that describe your product in addition to the main description. These are single words or short phrases and could include the brand name, product name or other distinguishing details that are specific to the item.

If you are given this opportunity it is important to use it. Every time you use keywords whether it is in your title, your description or in a list of tags, the internal search engine of the website is more likely to show your listing.

Choosing the correct category

Choosing the right category for your product listing is crucial because many people will also navigate through a website by the categories provided. Sometimes this might be very easy when you are selling things like computers or books. In other cases you may need to investigate what categories other sellers have used to sell similar products.

For example, would a Micky Mouse Watch go into a category listing watches, a category for children or a category for memorabilia? In some cases adding your listing to multiple categories will result in additional charges.

To see which are the most successful categories for your product do a search on the website for your item or as close to the item as possible if you are selling something you make. This should show you a range of competitor listings and from there you will be able to decide which categories are the most popular and make a judgement about which one is right for you.

Summing Up

- How you price your product will be dependent on what you are selling, why you are selling and where you are selling it.

- You may need to factor in additional costs such as your time, the cost of materials and your listing fees to the final price you set.

- A good product description is made up of photographs, an accurate title, a well-written description, the right category and keywords, tags and phrases.

- Products should be photographed in good light and against a neutral background.

- Photographs should include important details such as brand badges and any wear and tear.

- You should always take the highest resolution photograph possible as this will give viewers the best possible image. You can resize photographs on a PC with Paint.

- The title of your listing must include all the specific details such as brand and product names.

- Thinking about who might buy your product and why will help you to create the right sort of product listing.

- You can find out what other words and phrases people use to find your particular products by using the Google Keyword Tool.

- People search for products by using the search facilities and by using category listings; therefore choosing the right category is very important.

Chapter Four

Managing Your Stock

If you start selling online by clearing the house of unwanted clutter you will soon realise that this is a finite source of things to sell. There are only so many unwanted gifts and things you'd want to get rid of. Therefore, unless you are simply planning to continue selling off unwanted or unused items as they come along, at some point you will need to consider the question of *stock*.

Stock refers to the items that you either buy yourself at a low price in order to sell at a higher price, or items you make or create yourself in order to sell. Every online seller will deal with some sort of stock, whether it is physical or digital. This chapter will look at all the places you can find stock and how to manage it when you have it.

Financing your stock

Before we look at the various places you can find things to sell we need to think about how you are going to pay for any stock you buy in. Depending on where you find your items and what they are, this may or may not be a large financial outlay. Regardless of whether this is the case or not, it is still something you need to plan for.

Chapter 3 was all about how you price the products you are selling. The difference between the cost to buy or make something and the price you sell it is your *gross profit* and it is out of this difference that you need to pay for things like listing fees.

Spending too much on stock will mean that you could end up losing money when you add in the other fees that most websites will apply. The cost of your stock is therefore very closely related to the way you price your product. Just because something costs you £10 doesn't mean that you can sell it for £15 unless that is the price it normally sells for.

'Stock refers to the items that you either buy yourself at a low price in order to sell at a higher price, or items you make or create yourself in order to sell.'

If you visit any shop you will see that the shelves are full of things you can buy. The shop will have bought them in large quantities to reduce the price they pay. For example, if I buy 200 of product X I may pay £1 per single item; if I buy 2,000 though, I may pay as little as 20p per item. However, in order to buy 2,000 of these products I will need to spend £400 before I have made any money at all. This is what is meant by a financial outlay. I am speculating that I can sell £400 worth of stock for more money than it cost me in a reasonably short period of time so that I am not out of pocket for too long.

Let's look at an actual example.

If you visit Amazon UK and search for my book *LinkedIn Made Easy* you will see that a paperback copy sells for £10.28, although its list price is £10.99 (accessed 15th May 2013).

If I buy copies of this book from the printer to sell myself I pay £3.76 per copy plus £2.99 post and packing, although I can get them slightly cheaper if I buy more than 20 copies at a time.

Therefore the cost price of one copy of *LinkedIn Made Easy* is £6.75.

The retail price of the book is £10.99 and I generally sell them for £10 which means I make £3.25 profit on every copy I sell myself. If I were to sell my book for less than £6.75 I would lose money.

Knowing what an item will sell for and how much it costs to list it means you can always plan purchases of your stock to take these costs into account.

'Knowing what an item will sell for and how much it costs to list it means you can always plan purchases of your stock to take these costs into account.'

Housing your stock

When you find items to sell you will need to store them until they are sold. A couple of bookshelves or an empty cupboard may be all that is necessary for small items like books or CDs.

If you are selling larger or more fragile items then you may decide to devote some space in your home to your online selling activities. This could be a spare bedroom, unused dining room, conservatory, garage or even a shed – as long as it isn't damp. You can buy heavy-duty shelving from your local DIY shop which simply bolts together. Using archive boxes with lids means that your stock won't become dusty.

If you are making things to sell then you will almost certainly need some dedicated space to store raw materials and a place to make things up. This might mean turning a spare bedroom into a workroom.

Finding alternative suppliers

Just as there are lots of places to sell online, there are lots of places to find the stock itself. Sometimes it just takes a little lateral thinking.

If you started out by selling your clutter from the house you might decide that you would like to continue selling ad hoc items. The ideal place to locate such things would be charity and second-hand shops. However, you might also find something worth selling at local table top or jumble sales. Keeping an eye on the local parish magazine and free newspapers will reveal the dates of such events.

The disadvantage with this type of selling is that it can be a bit hit and miss and you may buy something that won't sell online because too many are already available or no one wants it.

If you get stuck with an item that hasn't sold you have just one option, which is to sell it for less than you paid for it to free up your storage space and your cash.

Therefore it may be more effective to specialise in one area and focus on that. For instance, you could focus on buying old DVDs, CDs, records, books or vintage clothes. Whilst they may not sell for huge amounts of money you know that choosing the right place to sell them will mean you can make small profits on each item.

The advantage of specialising is that you become familiar with what sells, how long it takes to sell and what the average price of an item is. This means you will probably take fewer risks with the money you have for stock and that your products will turnover much more quickly.

Using other retailers as suppliers of stock

It might seem a little odd to suggest using other retailers as suppliers of stock but in some cases it does work.

For example, I run an online site which specialises in women's health. We have a small online shop that supplies specialist books. In many cases it is cheaper for me to buy these books from Amazon and other high street retailers of low-cost books than it is to buy them from book wholesalers. This is because I only buy small quantities at a time, perhaps one or two of each, and either the wholesale companies won't supply in such small quantities or they have prohibitively high postage charges.

Similarly, eBay has a section for wholesale and job lots where it is possible to buy a large number of items ranging from baby clothes to Christmas cards.

Digital stock

'There are many advantages to selling digital goods. The biggest benefit is that one digital item can be sold many times in lots of different places.'

There are many advantages to selling digital goods such as music tracks, photographs and e-books. The biggest benefit is that one digital item can be sold many times in lots of different places. In most cases these items will be created by individuals and therefore you won't have any costs associated with purchasing items to sell.

However, they do need to be stored and a sensible directory structure on a computer will help make sure they are easily found when needed.

I have a folder on my computer which is called Books; this folder is subdivided into book titles and each subfolder contains all the files I need for each book including the text, images and different versions. When I need to work on a book or find a file I know exactly where it is.

One of the risks when creating digital goods is you can lose them if the computer crashes. A *back-up facility* such as Dropbox (www.dropbox.com) helps to prevent problems. This service allows users to store and update copies of files automatically. They have different types of accounts and in most cases the basic account is always free.

On-demand products

On-demand services fall into two categories. Services that sell things you create taking care of production and shipping for you. The other type of on-demand service is a website allowing people to set up a shop full of products with exclusive information, logos or images. They also take care of manufacture and shipping.

Both of these services mean it's possible to step outside the stock-holding loop altogether.

Typically these services provide a facility to open an account and sell a limited range of goods. The amount the buyer pays is set by the seller who can also buy items themselves at *cost price* to sell on other websites or direct to friends and family.

They may be called by different names like 'print on demand', 'publish on demand' or 'create on demand' and include sites like CafePress, Lulu, CD Baby.

My book, *LinkedIn Made Easy*, falls into this category as it is a print on demand product. Print on demand simply means that the book isn't printed until someone orders one or more copies. The same is true for all on-demand products.

CD Baby allows musicians to create CDs from their own music tracks. Customers can also order directly from CD Baby or sites like Amazon and the musician never has to make or send anything.

CafePress allows users to sell anything from T-shirts to mugs and even shower mats.

The advantage of selling on-demand products include:

- Knowing what the costs to buy the product are.

- Knowing what the selling price is because it's set by the seller.

- No stock, as there is an unlimited supply available, just when it's needed.

In some cases on-demand services even allow sellers to send an item directly to a customer who has bought elsewhere bypassing the need for sellers to handle the goods at all.

Drop shipping

Drop shipping is a term used to describe a process where a customer places an order for a product and someone else supplies it directly to them on the seller's behalf. The paperwork that accompanies the order comes from you and the customer is not aware that you haven't actually shipped and sent the products out yourself.

The advantage of drop shipping is that the seller chooses what price customers pay taking the difference between that and the cost the wholesaler sells to them as their profit. It means that sellers never have to carry large amounts of stock and don't get involved in the shipping or postage as that is all done for them.

It is a very similar process to on-demand except that the goods are already manufactured and are generally mass produced.

The disadvantage of drop shipping is the reliance on wholesalers fulfilling orders correctly and in a timely manner. One of the biggest complaints that most customers have is non-delivery or late delivery of things they have ordered. If you are interested in drop shipping you should research all of the companies thoroughly before signing up with any.

Some drop shipping companies will require the payment of a monthly fee to join their site. Others may charge a lot to post and pack orders for the end customer or set a minimum monthly transaction requirement. You can find out more information about drop shipping from The Wholesale Forums UK.

Becoming an affiliate seller

All sorts of online retailers offer something called *affiliate marketing* as a way of earning small amounts of money.

Each affiliate in a scheme is given a unique code identifying their specific account which is then embedded into product links. Those links can be shared on websites, in emails and through social media accounts with friends, family and acquaintances.

When someone clicks on one of these links and buys something from the site a small commission payment is deposited in the affiliate's account. Depending on the rules of the website operating the scheme, withdrawal of these earnings to a bank or PayPal account may not be possible until a certain amount has accumulated.

The advantage of becoming an affiliate is that it makes a small amount of money without having to make or find products to sell. There is usually no cost outlay to affiliates whatsoever.

The advantage to the company is that they only spend on advertising whenever someone buys a product thus avoiding the high costs of fixed adverts, TV and radio.

A search on Google for making money online will almost certainly reveal a number of different websites that recommend becoming an affiliate and they suggest that large amounts of money can be made doing so.

The reality is it's a difficult way to make any money because it relies on other people clicking on links you share and then buying from the website.

It really only works well for those individuals who have large mailing lists full of people who are eager to continue buying from a specialist or who have websites with lots of people visiting daily. Having said that, almost all large retail sites, Amazon and eBay included, run affiliate programmes which are free to sign up for.

Summing Up

- Selling unwanted items from your loft or garage only lasts for so long. If you are serious about selling online in the long term you will need to consider acquiring stock from other sources.

- The amount of money you pay for your stock is an important factor in how you price your products and you must do your homework to make sure you aren't paying too much.

- There are many alternative suppliers including charity shops, jumble sales and even high street retailers specialising in low-cost items.

- If you are buying things to sell you must be prepared to house them properly while waiting for a sale. Keeping things in one location will make it easier to manage.

- The biggest risk to digital items is losing them because your computer crashes. Registering for an online file storage solution like Dropbox will help to prevent this problem.

- On-demand services allow you to stock and sell unique items which you can order in small quantities when you need them.

- Drop shipping allows you to earn the difference between the price you sell an item at and the cost the wholesaler charges you. You do not have to get involved in shipping or holding stock as this is done for you.

- The biggest risk with drop shipping is orders not being delivered. You need to be sure that the wholesale company is reputable.

- Becoming an affiliate with a large retail company means you can earn money by providing links to their products in exchange for a small commission.

Chapter Five

Managing the Money

The reason most people sell online is to make money. They may be looking to earn a few extra pounds by selling things they no longer need or they may be looking to create a permanent extra income. In both of these cases it is important to manage the money. This chapter focuses on what is involved in earning money and taking payments online.

Upselling

It is important to remember that there are only four ways to earn more money as an online seller:

1. Sell more of the same product.

2. Sell lots of different products.

3. Sell existing products to new customers

4. Sell new products to existing customers.

When you visit McDonald's and place an order for food the assistant serving you will try to *upsell* to you by asking if you'd 'like fries with that' or by suggesting a larger size drink. Using the list above which of the four ways do you think McDonald's is using?

It is also possible to upsell to customers online and you will often see other items people are selling at the bottom of their listings.

For example, when I buy an image from Dreamstime I will be shown more images from the photographer. eBay, on the other hand, encourages you to select favourite sellers. Whenever a favourite seller adds something new to their listings an email is sent to all the buyers who have them listed as a favourite.

Upselling is often built into online selling websites already and therefore it's an advantage to have more than one item for sale as it increases the likelihood that a buyer may buy something else as well.

Understanding fee structures and associated costs

An important part of the online selling experience is learning how the site organises its fees and other associated costs.

Auction sites like eBay often have very complicated fee structures which comprise a listing fee for adding your product to their site, fees to emphasise your listing, such as the cost for additional photographs, and a final valuation fee which is paid when your item has sold.

'An important part of the online selling experience is learning how the site organises its fees and other associated costs.'

Before selling on these sites you will need to be sure of the fees and it is a good idea to check out all the documentation in advance of adding anything to the site.

Sites such as Amazon have fixed fees depending on the category the product is in. For example the selling fee for books is £2.40 and this is offset against the postage cost they credit to you.

Specialist or local classified listings often charge a small payment when creating the advert.

Finally, sites where digital goods are being sold build the fees into the system itself, paying creators the difference between the price they set and the cost to manufacture and ship.

Taking payments online

Some sites manage payments on behalf of their sellers. These sites include Amazon and those dealing with digital items. Most other auction and marketplace sites expect the seller to arrange payment themselves.

The most common way to take immediate payment by credit or debit card is to use a simple processing service such as PayPal or Google Wallet. These accounts are quick and easy to set up.

Payment processing companies do require users to go through a verification process to comply with international money laundering laws. This normally consists of depositing or charging small amounts of money to a bank account or credit card which, when confirmed, means the user becomes verified.

Almost all online selling sites will allow for the integration with one or more of the payment processing services discussed in this chapter. Which ones they work with will be dependent on who owns them and whether they have their own system or not.

The following information will be needed when setting up any payment processing account:

- Your name
- Your business name (if you have one)
- Your home address or registered address if it is a business
- Your VAT registration details if this is appropriate
- Your date and place of birth
- Your country of citizenship
- Your passport details
- A UK-registered credit card and valid billing address
- A UK-registered bank account in your name or your business name
- A UK landline number and possibly a mobile phone number

This information is needed to prevent online payment processing accounts being used for illegal purposes.

All the systems mentioned in this chapter are fully compliant with the legal requirements governing financial and banking organisations in the UK. They are all regulated by the FSA (Financial Services Authority) and have the required security in place ensuring their accounts are as safe as possible.

'The most common way to take immediate payment by credit or debit card is to use a simple processing service such as PayPal or Google Wallet. These accounts are quick and easy to set up.'

PayPal

PayPal was acquired by eBay in 2002 and is their preferred payment processor. It has two account types, personal and business. Either can be used to take payments from people online and both are free of charge to set up. There are no monthly fees associated with either of the basic accounts.

Customers don't need a PayPal account themselves in order to make a payment to sellers, however they will automatically create an account when they pay by credit or debit card.

A personal account is probably all that is needed for occasional sellers. Those who are planning to create an extra income by selling online in different places will probably need a business account. This is because it integrates with lots of different systems and allows sellers to send invoices to customers.

The basic fees for anyone selling goods up to the value of £1,500 each month is currently 3.4% of the transaction value plus 20p (accessed 21st April 2013). This means that selling something for £10 will incur a further charge of 54p and the PayPal account will be credited with £9.46.

The percentage charged can reduce to just 1.4% plus 20p per transaction as the level of monthly transactions increases.

A PayPal Pro account is useful for sellers who would like people to make payments over the telephone as well. The transaction fees are exactly the same as for the personal and business accounts but there is an additional £20 monthly subscription fee.

Withdrawals from PayPal to a bank account can be done manually at any time and amounts over £50 are free of charge.

Google Wallet

Google Wallet works in a very similar way to PayPal as customers can sign up for a Google Wallet account and use this to make payments to sellers. Google Wallet also allows account holders to make payments in a shop with just their phone.

There are no monthly charges for sellers using a Google Wallet account and the transaction fees are the same as PayPal at 3.4% plus 20p (accessed 21st April 2013) per transaction with reductions when selling more than £1,500 worth of goods each month.

The biggest difference between Google Wallet and PayPal is that Google Wallet automatically credits a bank account once a month.

Customers do not need to have a Google Wallet account to make a payment to sellers, however a Google account will be created automatically when they make a payment by debit or credit card.

Skrill (Moneybookers)

Moneybookers is also known as Skrill. It offers online sellers the same opportunity to process credit and debit cards as both Google Wallet and PayPal. However their transaction charges are lower at 2.9% plus 20p for monthly transactions up to £2,500. These fees also reduce if you increase the amount of money transacted in a month.

They also operate a merchant gateway system which allows sellers to take payments over the telephone and to charge recurring payments, such as a monthly subscription fees, for €19.95 per month (about £16.89 accessed 21st April 2013).

Nochex

Nochex offers two accounts: one for sellers only operating in the UK and one for those selling in the UK and abroad. The UK trader account limits individual transaction amounts to £100 and makes a transaction charge of 3.2% plus 20p. There are no monthly fees and withdrawals up to £500 can be made from accounts each day.

A Merchant Account allows transactions up to £1,000. It charges 2.9% plus 20p. There is a set-up fee of £50 to get an account and they negotiate a daily withdrawal limit.

'The biggest difference between Google Wallet and PayPal is that Google Wallet automatically credits a bank account once a month.'

Compare accounts

	PayPal	PayPal Pro	Google Wallet	Moneybookers	Nochex
Transaction charges	3.4% + 20p	3.4% + 20p	3.4% + 20p	2.9% + 20p	2.9% + 20p
Set-up charges	No	No	No	No	Yes
Monthly subscription	No	Yes	No	Yes	Yes
Transaction limits	None	None	None	None	£1,000
Request payments	Yes	Yes	Yes	No	No
Telephone payments	No	Yes	No	Yes	No
Send invoices	Yes	Yes	Yes	No	No
Recurring billing	Yes	Yes	No	Yes	No

Third party merchant accounts

Third party merchant accounts are used solely with *ecommerce* websites as they require integration with the software that runs them. They are typically used by online sellers who are dealing with large numbers of transactions on a daily basis.

Many of them charge monthly fees to use their service but they typically pay out to a bank account on a weekly or monthly basis.

The advantage of using a third party merchant account to process payments is that often they don't require customers to leave your website to complete their payment in the same way that simple services like PayPal do.

Checkout with Amazon

Checkout with Amazon is one of the easiest systems to set up as the account application process is very similar to that of PayPal or Google Wallet. Anyone that has an Amazon seller account can apply to use Amazon as their payment checkout as long as they have a website.

The biggest advantage of Checkout with Amazon is using the payment processing power of the largest online retailer in the world to charge customers through their Amazon accounts. There are probably few people in the UK who do not have an Amazon account.

However, it can only be used with sites where the products being sold are physical rather than digital. The transaction charges are 3.4% plus 20p for monthly sales up to £1,500. These reduce depending on how much you take through your shop.

WorldPay

WorldPay offers a number of different solutions for online sellers, including the ability to take payments from a website as well as over the telephone. There is a £75 set-up charge, a monthly subscription charge that starts at £15 per month and the transaction charges start from 1.95% plus 10p.

They make a charge of 35p when sending payments to a UK bank account and money is withdrawn to your bank account automatically one month in arrears on a weekly basis.

Minimising risks

One of the biggest risks an online seller has when processing payments online is that of fraud by buyers.

A few years ago, a relative of mine bought tickets for a concert through eBay and made the payment through PayPal. The tickets never arrived and by the time he realised it was a scam the PayPal account had been closed down and his money was never recovered.

I have also experienced a few occasions over the years where an order has been placed, a payment has been made and then the purchaser has claimed they never received the goods, forcing me to refund their payment.

'One of the biggest risks an online seller has when processing payments online is that of fraud by buyers.'

Most online payment processors operate a system that flags up whether a buyer is genuine. In other words they have a confirmed bank account, address and telephone number.

In PayPal this system shows up as a confirmed address in the order details. On Google Wallet this will show up under the Buyer Credit Verification on an individual order.

All payment processers require customers to add their billing address and the three-digit security number from the back of the card. Of course, having these details doesn't mean that the person using the card has the authority of the card holder to make payments.

If you are concerned about the possibility of fraud then it might be wise to insist that the delivery address for each item you are selling is the same as the billing address of the credit or debit card being used to make the payment.

Chargebacks

A chargeback is something that happens when a customer asks their credit or debit card company to reverse a payment they have made after it has been cleared. This can even happen where the item they have bought has already been posted to them. Sellers can challenge a chargeback on their account but the decision to uphold a customer complaint or not is in the hands of the card-issuing company.

The most common reason a chargeback is applied is because the goods weren't received. In most cases the buyer will try to contact the seller to resolve the problem, but if the seller refuses to respond then the buyer will often have no alternative but to ask their card company to claim back the payment.

Customers have 120 days after the expected delivery date to lodge a chargeback request.

The easiest way to avoid chargebacks is to communicate with customers whenever they get in contact. Using registered or recorded delivery means that sellers always have a proof of delivery.

Other payment options

Not everyone is comfortable paying for things online and it is still worth offering customers the chance to pay by cheque, cash or even over the telephone.

The number of buyers will almost certainly increase when they have more than one way to pay.

Cheque payment

Offering people the opportunity to pay by cheque means they need to receive clear instructions about who to make the cheque payable to, where they should send it and what will happen when it is received.

Waiting until a cheque has cleared before sending out the goods ordered means the problem of bounced cheques are avoided. Clearing a cheque can take as long as ten days with some banks.

Cash payment

If an item is bulky or large then it might be possible to allow buyers to collect it rather than posting it to them. It is common to ask for cash on collection in these circumstances.

The biggest risk with cash is counterfeit notes which are rejected by the bank when they are paid in. An alternative way to request a cash payment is to ask the buyer to deposit money directly into a bank account before collecting their purchase.

This can be done by giving them a bank account number and sort code. This is sensitive information and must be treated with caution and it might not be wise to share the details of personal bank accounts with new buyers who aren't already verified by their address or other details.

An alternative is to ask buyers to send money through a personal PayPal account. If they are based in the UK there will be no charges to either party and this can then be withdrawn to a bank account. Don't forget to ask the customer to sign a copy of their invoice when they collect the item.

'Not everyone is comfortable paying for things online and it is still worth offering customers the chance to pay by cheque, cash or even over the telephone.'

Telephone payments

Payments over the telephone by credit or debit card are illegal if sellers don't have a payment processing account that allows it.

An ordinary payment processing account must not be used as there are strict laws surrounding how such information should be processed and stored. PayPal Pro will allow you to take payments over the telephone as will Moneybookers and WorldPay.

Managing postage

Some sites like Amazon and those dealing with digital goods build the cost of postage into their fee structures. This means that sellers don't need to worry about this aspect of the sale.

Other auction and marketplace sites allow sellers to add an extra amount into the product description to cover the cost of packing and posting items to buyers.

It is important to factor in the cost of packing materials when deciding on postage costs. Is brown paper and bubble wrap needed or is a thick envelope good enough to send your goods?

Sometimes it is worth investing in specialist packing materials for DVDs and CDs. For example, a box of 100 bubble envelopes might cost around £13 to buy from a wholesale stationery supplier like Viking. Each envelope ends up costing 13p.

Is the post office local or will it involve a car drive and parking charges? It is surprising how quickly these costs can mount up and everything needs to be taken into account as it's very easy to find yourself out of pocket on things we take for granted.

Postage through Royal Mail is calculated on a size and weight basis and a pair of digital scales comes in very handy when working out the cost of postage. There is a handy postal cost calculator on the Royal Mail website at www.royalmail.com/price-finder.

Once the cost of packaging and the cost of postage has been added up this can then added to the product descriptions as your *shipping charge*.

Summing Up

- The fees to sell online vary from simple one-off costs to complex combinations of listing and final valuation fees.

- The cost of selling digital goods is often built into the sales system and sellers simply take the difference between the cost and their selling price as a commission or royalty fee.

- Fees to sell online can add considerable amounts of money to the cost of the items you are selling.

- Payment processing fees are another cost which must be taken into account when calculating the prices and they vary according to the service you are using.

- Offering buyers alternative options such as cheque payments can mean you attract buyers you might not otherwise have.

- Some online payment processing systems offer you the opportunity to take payments over the telephone.

- Buyers using a credit or debit card have the right to claim a chargeback up to 120 days after they may have received their goods.

- Sending out your orders with a proof of posting or recorded delivery receipt can minimise the risk of a chargeback being claimed.

- Shipping and postage costs are typically calculated on weight and size basis. Having a pair of digital scales will help to make these easier to work out.

- The cost of any packing materials, travel to the post office and parking charges must be taken into account when calculating postage charges.

- You can find a handy postal cost calculator on the Royal Mail website at www.royalmail.com/price-finder.

Chapter Six

Setting Up Shop

After you have been selling online for a while you may decide that it's time to set up your own online shop in addition to other online selling sites you are using.

This can often be a more cost-effective way of selling products and services, and it is even possible to sell a small number of products in your own shop completely free of charge, apart from the payment processing fees. Before taking this step however, there are a number of things to consider.

Business names and website addresses

Business names are no longer registered in the UK unless they are for a limited company and it is unlikely that most small online sellers will need to do this. Having a chat with an accountant as the business grows can help to make the decision about when to change your business status.

Just because business names don't need to be registered doesn't mean any name can be used. Some names may be protected legally as they are brand names and it's advisable to do an online search to see if anyone else is using it first.

The rules are pretty straightforward, unless the name is a registered trade mark or a registered company then you can use it, though it is wise to avoid the names of businesses selling the same things. The Companies House website provides a search facility for registered companies.

Having decided on a business name it is necessary to register a website address (domain name). A domain name is the bit of a web address after the www. For example internet-mentor.co.uk is the domain name for my limited

'Unless the name is a registered trade mark or a registered company then you can use it, though it is wise to avoid the names of businesses selling the same things.'

company, Internet Mentor Limited. Ideally, a domain name should include the business name but this may need a little lateral thinking to find something that works and is available.

You can check and buy available domain names on many different websites and I have listed a number of UK domain name registering companies in the help list at the back of the book.

When buying a domain name you will be prompted to buy some hosting, however this isn't always necessary.

Hosted and self-hosted online shops

There are two types of online shops, self-hosted or hosted.

A self-hosted shop is one where you buy some hosting space then find and install the software to run the shop. It is up to you to keep the site safe and secure and remember to update the software when required.

The costs involved in running a self-hosted shop include:

* Domain name registration, renewable every two years typically.

* Hosting charges. This is about £100 per year.

* Software costs, if any.

Although there are many simple solutions it is not an easy option and probably not the ideal solution for a beginner.

A hosted shop is where another company provides all the software and a selection of templates for the website. You simply add your domain name and the details of the things you are selling and hey presto – you have a fully working shop. They can be set up in a matter of hours. They have no long-term contracts and you can close them down quite easily and quickly should you need to do so.

The costs associated with a hosted shop include:

* Domain name registration.

* Monthly subscription fee to use the service. These start at about £15.

I have tried different versions of both these solutions and have found the easiest to manage and maintain is the hosted shop. This is why I use them for all the shops I manage today.

A good example of a hosted online shop is the one I have on The Hysterectomy Association website and you can see it by visiting http://shop. hysterectomy-association.org.uk.

The advantage of a hosted shop is that the shop owner can concentrate on selling products without worrying about the technical aspects of running what is actually a very complex website.

Most of them have a simple wizard system that walks users through the basics of getting started. They also have extensive online libraries of advice sheets about the different aspects of running the shop.

Creating an instant shop

Hosted shops could also be called instant shops because they can be up and running within a just a few hours of getting started. They have some common advantages which allow sellers to:

※ Easily add new products to their shop.

※ Present a consistent layout to customers that show product pictures and a description together with an *Add to Cart* button.

※ Set stock levels for individual products and in some cases variations for size and colour too.

※ Choose from a variety of postage options ranging from free and fixed cost to weight based.

※ Choose which countries to send orders to.

※ Choose which payment provider to use.

※ Let customers create accounts making it easier for them to shop next time as the store remembers their details.

※ Print out invoices and packing slips for orders.

※ Create special offers with coupon codes and discounts.

'The advantage of a hosted shop is that the shop owner can concentrate on selling products without worrying about the technical aspects of running what is actually a very complex website.'

※ Customise the shop with UK-based default settings such as the £ sign.

BigCommerce

The hosted shop I use for the Hysterectomy Association is provided by a company called BigCommerce which is based in Australia. They offer a 15-day free trial. Their monthly charges start at $24.95 (about £16.38) for 100 products.

Shopify

Shopify is based in the United States. It offers a free 14-day trial and their monthly charges start at £19.

The biggest difference between Shopify and other instant shops is that they also charge a transaction fee for each product bought through the shop, this starts at 2%.

Ecwid

A slight variation on the instant shop is one called Ecwid. This is unusual as it sits within an existing website. It has all the features of other instant shops and you manage your own store by logging in to the main site at www.ecwid.com. When you make a change on your account it is automatically reflected on the shop that sits in your website.

It is the ideal solution for anyone who already has a website and who wants to add a shop quickly and easily.

An example of an Ecwid shop can be found on the Internet Mentor website; visit www.internet-mentor.co.uk and click on 'Bookshop'.

Ecwid is free of charge if there are fewer than 10 products and if there is no need to have special offers or discounts. More products and functions has a cost of $15 per month (about £10).

Choosing the right design for your hosted shop

When you have decided on which service you would like to use for your hosted shop, the first task is to choose a template. A template is what allows all the pages and products in your shop to be displayed consistently on computers and mobile devices. A big advantage of the template system is that it is easy to give the shop a fresh new look.

Most online shops, including Amazon and eBay, have a very similar layout that provides product images, a description, an *Add to Cart* button and an area for any other information such as technical specifications. They will probably have a menu of links on the right or a left hand side and a menu of links above or below the logo at the top.

Colours are particularly important because they convey a huge amount of information to the customer. Darker and more muted colours like blue, black and grey tend to be associated with websites that appeal to men whereas lighter, brighter colours are used for websites primarily designed for women. Sites for children tend to have bold primary colours.

Each service will have its own systems and it is important that you read the documentation carefully.

Communicating with your customers

Most online shops will have a standard set of emails that are sent out to customers including:

- Order confirmations sent when an order has been placed and a payment method chosen.

- Payment confirmation sent when an order has been paid for.

- Shipping confirmation sent when the shop owner confirms the order has been posted.

In addition to these basic email messages a customer will also be informed when an order is cancelled or changed in some way. It is common practice to send a similar set of emails to the shop owner telling them when a new order has been placed.

'A big advantage of the template system is that it is easy to give the shop a fresh new look.'

In most cases you can customise these emails to contain more information or to add a personal message at the end.

Each email sent out will allow the recipient to reply to the email. This forwards a message to the store owner. It is very important to keep your customers informed in a timely manner about their orders. If an order won't be posted for a few days then it is important to let customers know. This reduces the likelihood of complaints, refund requests and chargebacks.

Setting store policies and compliance

The UK has strict legal policies in place that govern online selling. These can be found in the Electronic Commerce (EC Directive) Regulations 2002 and the Consumer Protection (Distance Selling) Regulations. According to the regulations the minimum information an online shop has to supply is:

'The UK has strict legal policies in place that govern online selling.'

- The official business name.
- An email address.
- The postal address of the business. If this is your home then you must add your home address.
- The registered company number and registered address if you are a limited company.
- Details of any professional or trade association you are a member of.
- The VAT registration number if you have one
- Prices must be clear and unambiguous and must state if they are inclusive of VAT or not. In most online selling situations the prices will always include VAT. The exception to this is if you are business who supplies other businesses that are registered for VAT.

Online sellers need to provide confirmation in writing of a buyer's purchase within seven days. They must give buyers seven days from the date they receive their order in which to cancel the contract and receive a full refund. Finally, they must ensure that buyers are protected against credit card fraud.

Hosted online shops and payment processing companies provide some of this legal compliance automatically through the written confirmation of orders and payment emails sent to buyers.

It is, however, up to the online shop owner to put together a set of terms and conditions which must include the following information:

- Details about how a customer can return the goods they have bought

- How refunds are dealt with

- The complaints procedure

- How a customer should contact the shop owner

If you do not have these policies in place then you may be fined.

In addition to these legal requirements, the UK's Data Protection Act requires that shops keep customer's personal information safe and secure. In practice this means that shop owners don't share customer details with anyone except where it is necessary to fulfil their obligations as an online seller.

Shop owners also have a responsibility to make sure that anyone else they share information with, such as drop shippers who are supplying goods on their behalf, are also aware of their obligations.

As long as you only keep information for the purposes of fulfilling orders and you are not sharing it with a company outside the UK then you don't need to register with the Information Commissioner. If you use an instant shop that is based outside the UK then you may need to register.

It is important to note that all these regulations apply whether you are selling on your own online shop or someone else's, like eBay.

The Business Link Helpline provides information about how to write a set of terms and conditions and privacy policies. Their number is 0845 600 9006.

Additional benefits of instant shops

Once your hosted shop has been set up you may want to consider some of the additional integrations that many of the services offer.

Perhaps the most important one will be with Google Analytics. This is a free service provided by Google which tells the account holder all sorts of information about who visits their website, how long they stay and which pages they visit. The biggest benefit of integrating Google Analytics is that it helps you to understand what is effective in your shop and what could be improved.

There are many tutorials about how to use Google Analytics available free online and setting up an account is very simple. Visit http://analytics.google. com in your web browser to get started. Once you have set up your account you will need to copy the unique code you are given into the right page on your shop's admin panel. There will be instructions about how to do this on all of the hosted shop sites.

Another integration many hosted shop services provide is with Face-book pages. Face-book pages allow a business to have a place on the main Face-book website which is not a personal profile and not part of the person-to-person interaction that takes place on the network.

You can have a look at www.face-book.com/LindaParkinsonHardman for ideas about how a Face-book page can be used to talk to your customers and fans.

You will also see a tab on this Face-book page which says 'Shop'. This is integrated with the hosted shop service Ecwid and it allows people to buy my books through my Face-book page instead of visiting my website.

To set up your own Face-book page visit www.face-book.com/pages/create and follow the onscreen instructions.

Summing Up

- Having their own online shop is the next logical step for people who are selling online on a regular basis.

- The first step to setting up your own online shop is deciding on a business name and then buying a domain name (web address).

- Online shops can either be hosted by the owner or hosted by an online ecommerce provider like BigCommerce, Shopify or Ecwid.

- If you host your own shop you will need to pay for hosting, as well as find and manage the software that runs the shop. This takes time and knowledge to implement.

- If you use someone else to host your shop you will pay a small monthly fee but can have a functional shop within just a few hours of creating your account.

- Most hosted shops cost from £10 a month to use, there are no long-term contracts and you can close them down whenever you want.

- Hosted shops use a template system to manage the design of the shop allowing you to focus on selling your products rather than learning technical skills.

- It is important that you keep in contact with customers. Most hosted shops will build these emails into their templates and they are sent automatically. You can often customise what they say.

- Selling online is heavily regulated and you will need to comply with the Ecommerce and Distance Selling Regulations and the UK Data Protection Act. These rules apply whether you are selling on your own shop or on sites like eBay.

- You can use a free service called Google Analytics to understand more about the statistics that relate to your shop visitors and their actions.

- Many hosted ecommerce solutions will integrate with Face-book pages giving you the chance to sell your products to people who 'like' your page on Face-book.

Chapter Seven

Marketing Your Products

Adding the listing is just the first, albeit very important, step in helping other people find products and services you are selling. Chapter 3 looked at promoting products by creating the right type of listing using titles, descriptions, photographs and keywords or tags.

This chapter will explore things you can do to put your listing in front of the right person to buy it.

Using the 4 Ps

The 4 Ps are the basis of many marketing strategies and they stand for product, place, price and promotion. In other words to sell something effectively, you must have the right product in the right place for the right price after effective promotion.

For example, WH Smith doesn't sell shoes; if they changed their mind, though, these would be the wrong products in the wrong place. We associate WH Smith with stationery and media like books or CDs.

The same expectations about where to buy things are used online as well. eBay is known as the place to buy second-hand items and Amazon is the place to buy books and CDs. And I wouldn't sell baby clothes on the Hysterectomy Association shop because the people that use the shop aren't looking for that type of item.

In chapter 2 we considered the various places you could sell your products and services online. Knowing the right place to sell your particular item is essential as it means that the audience visiting the site are already primed for the type of things you are selling.

'To sell something effectively, you must have the right product in the right place for the right price after effective promotion.'

In chapter 3 we also explored how you price products, learning that what other people charge for the same or similar items is a key element of our pricing strategy.

Customer feedback

One way of promoting products that you don't have to set up is customer feedback. Sites like Amazon allow other people to leave reviews about things they have bought and research shows that reviews can increase the number of sales for individual products (Do Online Reviews Affect Sales? Source: Social Science Research Network, accessed 10th April 2013).

On eBay this takes the form of feedback consisting of a seller rating. This feedback subtly tells other users whether someone is trustworthy.

'Research shows that feedback often contains product improvement suggestions.'

It is important to pay attention to the feedback customers leave for two reasons:

1. Because it shows where you might have problems with things e.g. delivery.

2. Because research also shows that feedback often contains product improvement suggestions, for instance it might say that people liked something but would prefer it in blue.

The second point is particularly helpful for those who make their goods by hand or who create digital products like music, videos or books. (Bazaar Voice Conversation Index, Source: Bazaar Voice, accessed 10th April 2013).

Social sharing

Social sharing is another popular form of customer feedback that gives people the opportunity to send a message to their Face-book and Twitter accounts, telling their friends and followers that they 'like' or have just bought or reviewed a product.

Setting up customer feedback systems

Customer feedback and social sharing is already built in to most online selling sites and when you create a new listing the icons will be included automatically somewhere on your product or service page.

If you are running your own online shop the software you choose may or may not make it available. If it is available you will almost certainly have to turn it on and instructions for how to do this will be contained within the help and support sections of your shop.

Spreading the word with social networking

There will be few people in the UK who have not heard of Face-book and even if you don't use it yourself you will almost certainly have friends or relatives who do.

The biggest advantage of a social network site like Face-book is that it allows people to chat to others about the things they are doing. They might share that they are in a particular shop or attending an event and, as we saw earlier, they may also tell people about things they have just bought.

However, social networking doesn't stop with friends talking to each other. It can also be used to spread the word about new listings that have been added to eBay or to show a picture of a new piece of jewellery on Etsy. It can even be used to share when a new book or music track is available to download.

Every time a piece of news is shared like this there is a chance that the people who see it will share it with their friends who in turn might share it with others.

The ideal outcome from any social networking site is that you start a conversation about the items you are selling with people who are interested.

The biggest social networks are:

- Face-book – Which primarily revolves around the people you already know.

- Twitter – Which allows you to follow conversations with people you don't know.

- Pinterest – Which shares pictures and videos of the things you like with others who have similar interests.

⊗ LinkedIn – Which is a business and professional-oriented network.

You will find a list of books to help you get started in the book list section.

Gifts, giveaways and competitions

We all like the word 'free' and giving away gifts or creating giveaways and competitions can help to attract the attention of people who don't know you yet.

This type of promotional activity works best for those who are selling things they make or create themselves. For example, a person making jewellery may offer a free pair of earrings when someone buys another product. They could also share on Face-book that they are running a competition where the winner will be the friend who has shared the details of a specific product on Etsy the most times.

Writers and authors can use the website Goodreads (www.goodreads.com) to create a giveaway of a new book they have written and musicians and photographers can offer some tracks or images free of charge on the sites they use to promote themselves.

Whilst it is difficult to find out whether sales increase as a result of doing activities like this, they do help to make products and businesses more visible. They do this by putting the business and products in front of people that don't yet know you with the chance that they will buy from you in the future.

Simple email marketing tactics

Without doubt, the easiest way to sell a new item is to someone who has already bought from you. They know you are trustworthy and will deliver what's been ordered.

Once a month I send an email to my mailing list telling them what has been going on with The Hysterectomy Association and about any new products we have. This activity always results in additional sales that I might not have received otherwise.

'We all like the word "free" and giving away gifts or creating giveaways and competitions can help to attract the attention of people who don't know you yet.'

Simple email marketing is built into many of the online selling sites. For example, when a favourite seller on eBay adds a product or if an author whose book I have bought on Amazon publishes a new one I will get an email message telling me.

You can also gather the first names and email addresses of people you have shipped goods to yourself, with their permission. For example, the Hysterectomy Association online shop has a facility to allow people to tick a box saying they would like to subscribe to a newsletter.

I also pop a flyer in the envelope for people who have bought from me through the Amazon marketplace asking if they would like to be added to my email newsletter and telling them how to sign up.

There are many opportunities for people to share their email address and it is always worth asking if they would like to be sent your latest news.

It is important to ask permission though, otherwise you will fall foul of the UK Data Protection Act 1998 and could be fined.

Depending on the numbers of people you are emailing you can do it with just a group of contacts stored in your email software such as Outlook or Gmail. When you have something to say you send one message to the whole group. If you have more than about 50 people on your newsletter list though, it might be worth using one of the online email management systems. Most of them offer a free account for a limited number of contacts.

You can find the links to some of the bigger and better systems in Appendix 3, Useful sites.

'Selling online doesn't mean that products can only be promoted online.'

Offline marketing tactics

Selling online doesn't mean that products can only be promoted online. There are all sorts of other actions you can take too. These include distributing leaflets to local households, taking business cards to events you attend or putting up posters on public noticeboards.

Don't forget to add the details of the product and how people can get it when making posters or leaflets. An email address or website and phone number gives readers more ways to get in touch to ask questions.

Applying the 4 Ps makes sure that leaflets or posters are only given to those people or put up in the places most likely to be interested in the products and services.

For example, a dog-walking service might put leaflets through people's doors, whereas a library poster would be perfect for selling second-hand books.

QR codes

Inevitably people reading posters won't have pens or paper handy to write down the details. The easiest way around this problem is to use a QR Code, you may have seen them on other leaflets you've received. They are a barcode that can be scanned by a smartphone. When they are scanned they take the person to a website.

Although QR codes sound complicated they are very simple to create and there are many online services that make them free of charge. Signing up for one of these accounts will also show the statistics that say when the QR code was used as well.

It is important to tell the software making the QR code where you want to send the person scanning it. This is usually a web page and ideally would be a specific product listing. There is a list of websites that create QR Codes in the Appendix 3, Useful sites.

Making search engines love your shop

Once you have been around the Web for a while you will come across the term 'SEO' or Search Engine Optimization. SEO is the art of persuading search engines to list your website or page as high as possible when someone does a search for a particular topic or product. This inevitably means Google, as it is the search engine with the largest number of users (Google Grabs More Market Share. Source: Search Engine Watch, 15th March 2013).

To see how a search engine works visit www.google.co.uk and type in the word 'hysterectomy'. You should see the Hysterectomy Association listed either first, second or third. This means every time someone goes to Google and types in that word I have a greater chance of them visiting my website rather than sites further down the page, even though those sites include the BBC and Bupa.

The reason the website is shown so highly is due to the following:

1. It is about a very specific topic related to the word that was typed into Google.

2. Lots of people visit the website on daily basis.

3. Many of those people leave comments and join in discussions there.

If you have a listing on a popular site such as Etsy, Amazon or eBay then you have a greater chance of showing reasonably high up the search engine page.

For example, if you go to Google and type in 'LinkedIn Made Easy' you will see that it shows the Amazon book listing at the top of the results.

'The most common online advertising system is called Google Adwords.'

Those starting out with a brand new website probably won't have the advantage of lots of visitors and will need to work on step one by writing lots of topic-related information. They then need to work on step two by encouraging people they know to search for and visit the website on a regular basis. One way to do this is through the use of competitions, free gifts and giveaways.

To learn more about SEO, see *SEO:The Essential Guide* (Need2Know).

Online advertising

The most common online advertising system is called Google Adwords and you will probably have seen adverts on the right-hand side of the search results when you use the Google search engine.

This and similar systems are called 'pay per click advertising' meaning that payment is charged only when someone actually clicks on the advert. The cost of each click can range from just a few pence to tens of pounds depending on what is being promoted and where it is linking to.

Every advert created on Google Adwords must have these characteristics:

▪ A headline that makes it stand out

- A short description of no more than 70 characters including spaces

- A link to a webpage preferably a specific item

Each advert is shown whenever one of the keywords or phrases I have chosen is typed into Google.

If you would like to try out Google Adwords many computer magazines have regular coupons for up to £100 free credit.

Summing Up

- Promoting your products and services is about more than just creating the right listing.

- Using the four Ps makes sure you have the right product in the right place at the right price following the right promotional activity.

- The simplest method of promotion is through customer feedback. This is automatically turned on in most online selling sites.

- Many online selling sites allow customers to show they 'like' a product on social networks like Face-book and Twitter.

- You can use Face-book and Twitter to tell friends and followers when you add new products to your online shops or sites.

- Gifts, giveaways and competitions are great ways to encourage people who don't know you to visit your online shop and listings.

- The easiest way to increase the number of sales you make is to sell to people who have already bought from you. The best way to do this is by sending them a regular email newsletter, although you must get their permission to do this first.

- You can also promote your products and services locally with posters, leaflets and business cards.

- QR codes mean that people can easily get the details of a product or service from a poster or leaflet on a noticeboard with just a smart phone.

- You can encourage the search engines to show your products and services if you write about the topic regularly.

- You can advertise online through Google Adwords for specific words and phrases. These adverts cost from a few pence to several pounds to buy.

Chapter Eight

Selling On Amazon

Amazon is the largest online marketplace in the world catering to millions of people and selling everything from books to camping gear. It is also offers one of the biggest opportunities to sell to a large and varied audience. In this chapter we'll be exploring how you can tap into the mighty Amazon retail machine.

There is a lot of information available on the Amazon website about how to use all of the services discussed in this chapter and links have been provided in the help list.

Amazon Marketplace

If you have an item to sell, be it a book, a CD or an archery set; as long as it is mass produced and already listed then you can sell yours in the Amazon Marketplace. There a few exceptions to this which are mostly related to manufacturers selling their own products.

Before starting there is one fundamental principle that must be understood first. Amazon creates one page for each product available on its site. All sellers offering the same product are added to the same product page.

Why not visit Amazon UK now and find the details of a book or a CD you have recently bought.

The number of new and used sellers of that item will be shown below the main product details. These are also listed as 'More Buying Choices' on the right-hand side of the product details page.

Underneath 'More Buying Choices' there is a link to 'Sell Yours Here'. Getting started is as simple as clicking the link and completing the details requested.

'Amazon is the largest online marketplace in the world catering to millions of people. It also offers one of the biggest opportunities to sell to a large and varied audience.'

One of the biggest advantages of the Amazon Marketplace is that you don't have to create a listing yourself because that has already been done for you. All you need to do is select the condition of the item you're selling, enter the price you want to charge, the number you have to sell and say if you are prepared to send it to countries outside the UK.

If you don't have an account, you will be prompted to create one on the next page; or you can do so by signing in with the same account details you use to buy from Amazon.

When you have a Marketplace account you have access to a sales dashboard which allows you to monitor your inventory (the products you are selling), your sales and payments from Amazon.

Payments are made directly to the bank account you nominate every 14 days, and you can request payment whenever you want once you have received the first automated payment.

'Pricing on the Marketplace is a composite of the price you set plus the shipping allowance that Amazon gives you.'

Pricing on Amazon Marketplace

Perhaps the biggest disadvantage of using Amazon Marketplace is that you won't be able to offer free shipping which is standard across everything that is supplied by Amazon themselves.

You will also need to remember that people tend to use Amazon Marketplace sellers where they are cheaper overall and have a good seller rating.

Pricing on the Marketplace is a composite of the price you set plus the shipping allowance that Amazon gives you. You will be charged a fee when your item sells and these vary according to the category.

For example, *101 Handy Hints for a Happy Hysterectomy* retails at full price for £7. It costs about 90p to print (this is the base cost) therefore the profit margin when it's sold through the association website is £6.10.

Amazon currently sells copies for £6.30 including post and packing. To match this I must ensure that the cost to the purchaser, including the cost of shipping, is less than £6.30 if I want them to buy from me instead.

- Home & Garden

- Toys

If you have a Pro Seller Account you can sell your own items in all the Amazon categories. Although, if you are selling clothing, jewellery, health and beauty, groceries and watches there is an an approval process before products are displayed.

You will need what is called an EAN (European Article Number) for the product you are adding to the catalogue. This gives you a unique barcode for your product and allows you to sell it in any online marketplace.

In the UK, the organisation responsible for handling EAN codes is GS1 UK. You will need to become a member first and this costs from £107.

Fulfilment by Amazon

The key to making a sale on Amazon is to say you can post within 24 hours (except Sundays and bank holidays). This standard is expected by buyers using the system and means you must be available to post your items when something is sold.

The easiest way to achieve this is by using the Fulfilment by Amazon service. Not only does it mean your items are posted in the 24-hour time frame but they are also sent free of charge to the buyer, reducing the cost and making it more attractive.

It is best used by those online sellers who are selling large quantities of goods through Amazon rather than the casual clutter-clearer, because of the costs involved.

Fulfilment by Amazon users cover the cost of sending their items to Amazon's warehouse and then pay fees for storage, packing and handling on top.

For example the 74p cost associated with using Fulfilment by Amazon for a £10 book is broken down as follows:

- Order Handling per order – 1 order x £0.00

- Pick & Pack per Unit – 1 Unit x £0.50

- Weight Handling – £0.23

'The key to making a sale on Amazon is to say you can post within 24 hours (except Sundays and bank holidays).'

▪ Storage Fee for 0.000616 cubic metre x £14.12 – £0.01

Kindle Direct Program

A Kindle is a device that allows people to read e-books they have bought and downloaded from the Amazon website.

The Kindle Direct Program provides authors with an opportunity to self publish their books specifically for the Kindle reader and other e-book enabled devices such as computers, tablets and smart phones with the Kindle App. It is one of the easiest ways to self publish. There are no third parties involved and the author is responsible for the quality and content of the book they sell.

It is free to join and the author sets the selling price of their book somewhere between 99c (about 66p) and $9.99 (about £6.62).

Books selling at $2.99 (about £1.98) or over receive a 70% royalty payment every time they are sold. Books selling at less than $2.99 receive a 35% royalty payment for each one sold.

There is a lot of debate amongst authors about what price to set and obviously higher prices mean fewer book sales. For a well-known author this is probably not an issue. For someone starting out then using the lower price is a handy way of increasing the number of people likely to sample their work.

Creating a Kindle e-book

A Kindle e-book can be created from a basic Microsoft Word file that has removed all the special characters which don't convert correctly to e-book formats.

This file can then be uploaded to a Kindle Direct Program account and is converted automatically to the correct format for sale on Amazon. It is possible to check what it looks like on various devices through the built-in viewers.

A cover image is needed in addition to the file for the body of the book. This is displayed next to the title. It is worth remembering that we do judge books by their covers so it's worth spending time getting this right.

Once the book and cover have been uploaded, the geographic area for rights is selected. For most independent authors this will be worldwide and will mean that the book is available for sale on all Amazon stores.

Although *ISBNs* (International Standard Book Number) are not needed for a new e-book it must have one to sell on other e-book websites. UK ISBN numbers are purchased from Nielsen in batches of ten at a cost of £126 (accessed 25th April 2013).

The most important part of any Kindle listing is the description. This is very similar to the sorts of descriptions that would be used on sites like eBay and discussed in chapter 3.

The description must be relevant to the e-book. It must contain keywords if they are important and it must give the reader some sense of what they will be reading. Every new e-book can be added to two categories and with dozens to choose from it's possible to become very specific, right down to fiction featuring women detectives. Every listing can also add up to seven keywords.

The Kindle Direct Program pays all royalties to UK authors, regardless of the country in which an e-book was bought, in sterling. Credits are made directly to a bank account 60 days after the end of the calendar month when sales occurred, as long as the balance has reached £10.

Once the first payment has been received there are monthly credits, 60 days in arrears, as long as the balance is £10 or more.

Createspace

Amazon also has its own publishing company for paperback books, music and videos called Createspace.

Createspace allows creators of digital and written content to make their products available through Amazon stores on a *print on demand* basis. Whenever a paperback book or a CD is ordered through Amazon it is printed to order and posted to the customer.

The advantage of using this print on demand service is that there is no need to carry stock and no need to think about postage even though the products are for sale in the world's largest online marketplace.

'Createspace allows creators of digital and written content to make their products available through Amazon stores on a print on demand basis.'

In addition to these benefits, a distribution licence can also be added allowing authors, musicians and budding film directors to distribute their work to other online sellers in the United States. This is available at a cost of $25 (about £16.57).

Createspace has no set-up fees and it's possible to purchase your own products at wholesale cost for distribution yourself. They do take take a commission on everything sold through the system and currently these figures are:

- Books – 40% of the cover price
- CDs – $4.95 (about £3.28) + 45% of the cover price
- DVDs – $4.95 (about £3.28) + 15% of cover price

Digital music and video can also be sold and Amazon pays a royalty of $0.65 (about 43p) for each music track sold and 50% of the purchase price set by the creator on downloadable videos.

These costs may seem high but when you bear in mind that once an item has been added to Createspace you no longer have anything else to do they seem much more reasonable.

Amazon Associates

The concept of affiliate income is discussed in the section in chapter 4. As you might expect from the world's largest retailer, Amazon have an excellent affiliate system in place and you can sign up using your usual Amazon account details by visiting http://affiliate-program.amazon.co.uk.

Once logged in, a grey bar appears across the top of every page of the Amazon website. This is where quick links to any item on Amazon containing your personal affiliate code can be created quickly and easily.

Affiliates earn what Amazon calls advertising fees, these are a percentage of the amount a person using one of their links spends on the various Amazon websites.

Affiliates are paid by direct deposit or Amazon.co.uk gift certificate 60 days after the month end when there is a balance of £25 in the account. It is possible to be paid by cheque but this requires an account balance of £50.

Summing Up

- You can sell unwanted items easily through the Amazon Marketplace, simply log in to your usual Amazon account and use the 'Sell Yours Here' button if it's available.

- You must price your stock carefully when using Amazon Marketplace because you will have to fund the cost of sending your item to the buyer out of the money you receive.

- Every Amazon Marketplace seller has their own free website showing all the items they are listing in one place.

- You can sell handmade items on Amazon but you will need a European Article Number which you can get from GS1 in the UK.

- To increase the likelihood of someone buying your product you may want to take advantage of Fulfilment by Amazon, a service they provide which allows your products to be stocked in their warehouses.

- Authors can take advantage of the Kindle Direct Program which allows them to make their books available as Kindle e-books and earn up to 70% in royalty payments.

- Musicians, authors and video makers can use Createspace to sell their books, CDs and DVDs on the Amazon store as a print on demand product or as downloadable versions.

- Createspace also offers people making digital goods the opportunity to sell in other online outlets and libraries across the United States.

- Amazon offers an affiliate selling program called Amazon Associates. It allows anyone with an Amazon account to sign up and earn a small amount of money by sharing links to products and pages with their friends and family.

Chapter Nine

Selling On eBay

If you were to ask anyone in the street where they would sell their unwanted items online, the chances are they would say eBay without a moment's hesitation. It is the largest online auction site in the world and in the UK they estimate that 178 million people use eBay to run a business or provide a main or second source of income (eBay Company Overview. Source: eBay.co.uk, accessed 22nd May 2013).

It is a great place for people to start online selling because it allows them to understand the processes involved as well as develop the necessary skills for use in other marketplaces as well.

Setting up your account and getting started

New sellers need to register with the site and create a seller account. This account contains personal information such as their name, email, home address and telephone number. A valid credit or debit card is also needed to pay selling fees and any eBay buyer protection reimbursements. eBay also recommend setting up a PayPal account to accept payments online, and there is more about this in chapter 5.

Once the account is set up it is easy to get started. After logging in click the 'Sell' link that can be found at the top of most eBay pages. Depending on the category and listing form there are a number of options to choose. Reviewing chapter 3 before adding items will mean that things go into the right category.

The first listing a new seller creates is an auction item. An auction allows people to bid on their item for the number of days they decide and the highest bidder wins the item. The reason for this restriction is because in order to sell a fixed price item sellers must have a feedback score greater than 0.

'In the UK they estimate that 178 million people use eBay to run a business or provide a main or second source of income.'

Feedback

What is feedback?

Feedback is an indicator of online reputation as both a buyer and a seller. It is a score automatically calculated from comments and ratings left by other members you have bought from and sold to. The score is included in your feedback profile.

How feedback works

Buyers and sellers can choose to leave a rating and a comment for every transaction they conduct.

Feedback from buyers consists of a positive, negative or neutral rating and a short comment.

'Feedback is an indicator of online reputation as both a buyer and a seller.'

Feedback from sellers can only consist of a positive rating and a short comment. These ratings are used to determine the overall score. With some exceptions feedback works like this:

- A positive rating increases your feedback score by one point.
- A neutral rating does not change your feedback score.
- A negative rating decreases your feedback score by one point.

Each member that leaves feedback can affect the overall score by one point (positive, negative or neutral) for each transaction they completed.

Only registered members can leave feedback and it's important to remember that comments are very difficult to remove once they have been left, therefore being specific, fair and factual is always recommended.

It's normal to assume that a high feedback score is a good indicator that the person is a trustworthy member, however it is always worth reading through the comments to see if any negative comments might have been left.

Resolving issues

With enough use every member on eBay will encounter an issue like non-payment from the buyer, non-delivery by a seller or negative feedback at some time. The important thing is to remain calm as eBay have systems in place which help to resolve problems as easily as possible. The next thing to do is get in touch with the buyer or seller to try and resolve the problem.

There are also a few things you can do to help prevent problems from happening in the first place.

Remember that communication is very important. For example, if there is going to be a delay sending an item to a winning buyer it is important to let them know and give them timescales. This way their expectations will be set at a level that can be met.

Almost all negative feedback stems from communication issues. If someone does leave negative feedback you can request that they change it through the eBay systems.

'Remember that communication is very important.'

If a buyer fails to pay for the item they have bought get in touch with them as soon as possible. There may have been an emergency they needed to deal with. If they don't respond to your email within a couple of days then their contact information can be obtained from eBay and a phone call can be made.

Payment reminders can be sent between two and 30 days after the listing has ended. If there is still no response then the unpaid item case system should be used which can be found in the eBay Resolution Centre. The buyer is notified immediately and has the opportunity to respond. If they don't reply or it's not possible to reach an agreement then the case can be closed and a credit can be received to cover the final valuation fee. Once a case has been closed the item can be relisted or offered to another bidder.

Setting up an About Me page

Reputation is extremely important on eBay, therefore you should always be thinking about ways to improve it. One of the best ways to do this is to create a memorable About Me page.

The About Me page is an opportunity to promote sellers and their listings and is free of charge to everyone with a user ID. However, many people don't bother to create their page and they are missing out on a valuable way to communicate with potential buyers. Sometimes people will buy from one person rather than another simply because they liked them more.

A good head and shoulder photograph of you smiling at the camera avoiding anything that others might consider inappropriate can be added to the page together with a phone number and address.

Adding this information goes a long way to establishing trust with those who don't yet know you because they feel confident they can see you and get in touch if there is a problem. Some people don't feel comfortable leaving such personal information openly online and if this is the case then it might be worth using a call forwarding service that forwards to your phone from an anonymous number. Some of these services are free of charge and you can find their details in Appendix 3, Useful sites.

An About Me page will also contain the details of feedback that has been received as well as any listings. Other modules such as a biography, a guest book so that visitors to your page can talk to you and any guides or reviews you have written can also be added. To create an About Me page click on your username after logging in to eBay and the page will appear, it can then be edited.

Understanding seller fees on eBay

As soon as something is listed for sale on eBay a fee is charged regardless of whether it sells or not. If it sells then a final valuation fee will also need to be paid.

How much these fees are depends on a number of different things including the starting price, whether it's an auction or fixed price item and the category it is added to.

Here are the fees explained in more detail:

- Insertion Fee – Creating a new listing using the 'sell your item' form will charge an insertion fee, this is based on the starting price of your item.

- Final Value Fee – If the item sells a final value fee based on the final amount it sells for, not including postage and packing costs, will be charged.

- Listing Upgrades – Highlighting a listing by adding extra photographs, using a subtitle or other enhancement will add small additional charges. The amount of each charge is dependent on the category and whether it's an auction or fixed price listing.

The fees can be reviewed before the listing is submitted. For example, currently the basic fees for selling a £10 book would be £1.10 for a fixed price item and £1.20 if it sells for £10 as an auction listing. One advantage of eBay is that postage and packing costs are charged in addition to the cost of the item, rather than as part of the item price.

Creating a listing on eBay

Starting a new listing can be quick and easy. Searching for an item with its correct name may reveal that it is already listed in the eBay catalogue. If this is the case then there may be a link underneath the product image saying 'Have one to sell? Sell it yourself' clicking this starts the listing process automatically.

In some cases, mostly for electronic equipment, it is only possible to use the product details supplied by eBay in a product listing.

The advantage of creating a listing in this way is that it will be listed in the correct category and will also show up with the other listings for the product too. Unlike Amazon, multiple listing pages can be created for the same item.

If an item isn't in the eBay catalogue then a listing must be created from scratch following the principles laid out in chapter 3 to create the ideal set of product details.

After selling on eBay you can use previous things that have been added as templates for new items. The same item can also be relisted if one happens to become available.

Fixed price listing, best offer or auction?

There are no hard and fast rules about which to use and the answer probably depends on what you are selling.

Fixed price listings are better for commodity items where lots of the same things are available to you or other sellers. They are also good for accessories to other things being sold like the mouse or case that goes with a laptop.

If the product has multiple options such as sizes and colours or where they belong to a wide selection of related items like car parts or specialised craft supplies, then these items are also ideal for fixed price listings.

The following criteria must be met before something can be sold as a fixed price listing:

- Have a feedback score greater than 0
- Accept PayPal as a payment method on your listing or been a registered user of eBay for more than 14 days

'Fixed price listings are better for commodity items where lots of the same things are available to you or other sellers.'

It is possible to use a 'best offer' option together with a fixed price listing. Best offer means that buyers can suggest a price they're willing to pay for the item. If it's acceptable the listing ends and the person making the offer wins it. Each best offer is only valid for 48 hours. The offer can be negotiated by sending a counter-offer to a buyer, here's how:

1. Go to the best offer console for the listing.

2. Select the best offer in question and click make a counter-offer.

3. Enter the counter-offer price and terms and click send.

A best offer and a counter-offer are binding, just like any other bid. However, sellers can make multiple counter-offers if they receive best offers from different buyers. The first buyer to accept the counter-offer will win the item.

Best offer isn't available for every category and sellers have to meet certain conditions to use the best offer system.

An auction listing is perfect for single items cleared from cupboards or wardrobes, unique or hard to find items, and a good strategy to adopt is to start with a low price to encourage viewers and bidders as a reserve price (the lowest price you are willing to accept) can always be set for a small additional cost.

The auction style format is very flexible and it can be combined with a 'buy it now' price so that anyone can choose to pay the asking price and end the auction immediately.

Depending on the selling options you select when you make your listing, additional fees may apply:

▨ Auction listing with a buy it now option – An insertion fee based on the starting price plus an additional fee for the buy it now option is paid. If there is a reserve price the insertion fee is based on that amount.

▨ Fixed price listing – An insertion fee based on the buy it now price is paid.

▨ Fixed price listing with a 'best offer' option – An insertion fee based on the buy it now price is paid. If the item sells at the best offer price the final value fee is based on the offer accepted.

Setting up an eBay shop

An eBay shop displays all a seller's listings regardless of their category and selling format in one central location. Shops have their own unique website address and this can be added to websites, emails, social networks, leaflets, posters and business cards.

A feedback score of at least 10 and a verified PayPal account is needed before a basic eBay shop can be opened.

Shops are not for everyone and those sellers with the best results will generally be more experienced and committed to increasing their sales to become a full or part-time business.

Every shop comes with five pages that can be customised with additional information. They also have cheaper insertion fees for fixed price listings.

There are different levels of eBay shop account which are determined by how much is being sold and the monthly subscription cost chosen. The basic shop currently has a monthly fee of £14.99.

eBay classified ads

In addition to the auction and fixed price formats there is now the classified advert. These are similar to the type of advert found in local papers and are restricted to the following categories:

- Cars, Motorcycles and Vehicles
- Boats and Watercraft
- Campers, Caravans and Motorhomes
- Business, Office and Industrial
- Farm Implements and Equipment, Tractors
- Construction Tools, Lifting Tools, Woodworking, Saws
- Property
- Holidays and Travel, Accommodation

There is a single insertion fee and no final valuation fee. Fees start at £9.99 for something in Business, Office and Industrial and go up to £35 for a property.

Every advert placed through this system is shown on eBay for 28 days.

Summing Up

- Setting up an eBay account is very simple, you just share your personal details and add a credit or debit card to pay their fees.

- You can sell on eBay in an auction format or for a fixed price. If you are new to eBay then you must sell through an auction to gain some feedback before being allowed to sell items for a fixed price.

- Fees are based on the insertion fee and the final valuation fee. Additional fees are charged to add extra photographs or other features designed to make the product listing stand out.

- Auction formats are ideal for unique or hard to find items.

- Fixed price formats are ideal for commodity items, accessories and where you have lots of the same thing to sell.

- All eBay accounts come with a free About Me page which allows you to tell potential buyers more about yourself and display your listings in one place.

- Feedback is very important on eBay and is used as a way of establishing the credibility and reliability of both buyers and sellers.

- Most issues that result in negative feedback are caused by poor communication. If problems do arise, eBay has a number of different systems and procedures in place to help you resolve them.

- You can set up a shop on eBay for a small monthly payment. This allows you to list your items in one place and you can share your unique shop web address on your own website, on business cards, emails and leaflets.

- Classified ads on eBay allow you to list a car, motorhome, boat, tools, property or holiday for 28 days for a fixed price.

Chapter Ten

Tax and Legal Implications

The most important thing to remember when selling online is that lack of knowledge cannot be used as a defence in court should anything ever get to that stage. It is the responsibility of all online sellers to know how the law affects them and what they must do to comply with tax requirements. This doesn't need to be difficult and a few simple actions taken on a regular basis will ensure you avoid possible problems in the future.

If you are simply selling items that you no longer need on an occasional basis then the chances are that much of what is discussed in this chapter won't apply to you. In these circumstances the best advice is to keep receipts for everything, that way you can prove that the item you are selling is genuinely something you no longer needed.

Even if you think this chapter doesn't apply to you it is worth reading, as there are some things everyone selling online needs to be aware of.

'It is the responsibility of all online sellers to know how the law affects them and what they must do to comply with tax requirements.'

Tax

If you are planning to use online selling to supplement your income then you will need to register with the HMRC (HM Revenue and Customs) for *Self Assessment*. This means that part of your income will be as someone who is self-employed. You can be employed and self-employed at the same time and you will be sent an additional tax return form to complete each year in addition to any tax you pay through the PAYE scheme of an employer. You can find out more about registering with the HMRC here: www.hmrc.gov.uk/sa/self-emp.htm.

Most online sellers will start out as a sole trader. This is the simplest type of business and it is perfectly legal to run a business and be employed at the same time. If you want to form a limited company instead you should hire an accountant to do the more complex accountancy work required for corporation tax.

You will also need to save some of your profits each month to pay your additional tax bill. Tax is payable at the current rate on income over and above the taxable allowance. If you are employed then your taxable allowance will almost certainly be used up by your employer and you will pay tax on everything you earn from selling online. Self-employed income tax is due to be paid before 31st January each year and fines are levied if this date is not met.

For example if your taxable allowance is £5,000 and you earned £12,000 you would pay tax on the difference between the two which is £7,000. If you earn £12,000 from an employer and have a profit of £5,000 from online sales then you have earned £17,000 and tax would be payable on £12,000.

Tax for the self-employed is calculated a year in arrears. Whatever you earn between the 5th April 2013 and the 4th April 2014 will result in a tax bill to pay before 31st January 2015.

You can find out more about the current tax rates and allowances on the HMRC website.

VAT

If a business earns more than the VAT threshold in a year it must register to pay VAT (£79,000 in 2013-14. Source: Gov.uk/vat-registration, accessed 21st April 2013). The amount of VAT paid or claimed back from the HMRC is determined by the difference between the VAT charged to customers and the VAT paid on purchases.

You can register for VAT online on the HMRC website. Alternatively you might find it more helpful to hire an accountant who can manage your accounts, annual tax and VAT returns for you.

National Insurance

Online sellers who are using this as way of regularly supplementing their income also need to pay additional Class 2 National Insurance contributions on anything they earn over the annual limit for registered self-employed people.

In the 2013-14 tax year the limit is £5,725 (Source: HMRC, accessed 21st April 2013). This applies regardless of whether you are employed or not.

Simple bookkeeping

All earned income is liable for tax in the UK. This includes income from anything sold online unless they are things you have owned for sometime but no longer want.

It is good practice, even for occasional sellers, to keep the receipts for everything bought and a record of the date it was sold. This is because if you are investigated by the Inland Revenue they will need to see proof that what you sold was indeed something you no longer wanted, rather than something you bought specifically to sell.

The minimum records required are:

- Sales records
- Purchase records
- Bank statements

Sales records

These are the details of each item sold online. Most online marketplaces and online shop software allow sellers to print out a copy of each invoice. These can then be filed with a proof of posting or recorded delivery receipt from the post office in date order.

Some sites will also allow the download of sales and orders into a spreadsheet program such as Microsoft Excel. This is an excellent way to keep a *back-up* record should you decide to change sites or systems.

If you are using an online payment provider like PayPal, you will also be able to download the details of any financial transactions that take place.

Purchase records

Purchase records are made up of everything that is bought to run a business. This will include any stock, equipment like cameras or computers, consumables such as paper and ink cartridges, packing materials, postage and monthly fees.

It is important to keep all receipts, even for cash purchases. They are necessary to prove that money was spent on that item and therefore is an expense you can claim against tax.

'It is good practice to open a new bank account for your business unless you are only selling items you no longer want.'

The fees for processing payments online through sites like PayPal are deducted before a bank account is credited and therefore don't necessarily need to be accounted for. However, they are still a purchase and you may want to keep a record of them.

A self-employed tax bill will be calculated on the difference between the amount taken in sales receipts or transferred to your bank account and the amount paid for business purchases.

Bank statements

It is good practice to open a new bank account for your business unless you are only selling items you no longer want. This will make it easier to sort out your accounts every year as you will be able to see exactly what you have earned and what you have spent. You can do this with the same bank that holds your personal account or any other bank.

Each month you should check your bank account to make sure that the money you received is what you expected and that you have receipts for every purchase.

Simple bookkeeping software

If you are happy to manage your accounts yourself and are selling only a few items then you can set up a very basic spreadsheet in Microsoft Excel. You can use one sheet to record your sales with information such as:

* Date sold

* Item sold

* Amount received

* Postage cost

* Customer name

* Customer contact details

You will then need a separate sheet in the same file to record your purchases with the following information:

* Date bought

* Item bought

* Item cost

You can then use your bank statement to tick off the items as they appear.

There is also simple software available that allows you to do more analysis of your accounts. It allows you to allocate your purchases to different types of category such as postage, consumables, expenses, etc. You can also keep a record of customers and how much they have paid you.

A list of the systems you can use can be found in Appendix 3, Useful sites.

UK distance selling regulations

The UK has a set of regulations that cover the buying and selling of goods and services without face-to-face contact. They cover shopping online, by mail order, telephone or television. The Consumer Protection (Distance Selling) Regulations give consumers legal rights when they buy goods from a trader who normally sells goods or services at a distance.

It doesn't matter how someone pays for the goods, and the regulations apply to both new and second-hand goods.

The regulations do not apply to goods bought through an auction or online auction unless the purchaser used a 'buy now' function, rather than bidding.

All online sellers must comply with the distance selling regulations by providing the following information to purchasers:

* Full business name or own name if you don't run a business

* Geographical address

* Telephone number and an email address

* Details of any trade association membership, including a registration number

* Professional qualifications if selling professional services

* VAT number (if registered for VAT)

* How the customer is expected to pay

* Delivery information

In addition to this information, prices must be clear and include taxes and delivery costs and orders must be acknowledged as soon as possible, this is often automated in an online sales system.

Online sales sites like eBay and Amazon include these details in the automated systems that communicate with both buyers and sellers.

If you are selling through your own website you will need to add this information. If you don't add this information then you can be fined.

People buying online may also have the right to cancel their order within seven days this is known as a 'cooling off period'. In these circumstances you can request that the goods be returned to you at the customer's expense, but you must refund the cost of the item they bought within 30 days.

There are some exceptions to this right including:

* Personalised items or those made to order

* Newspapers and magazines

- Media or software where the security seal has been broken

- Perishable items such as flowers or food

- Items bought through an online auction on sites like eBay

- A new service that starts immediately such as access to a website

- Train tickets, hotel bookings, taxis or events to be delivered on a specific date

The government website has more information about the requirements that online sellers must meet on the GOV.UK website.

Creating terms and conditions

All websites that are selling online must have a set of terms and conditions and many online services like eBay will give you the opportunity to create one that can be used on each listing. People selling through the Amazon Marketplace do not need to worry about this as it is built into the website already.

Terms and conditions must include the information required to meet the distance selling regulations and must include information about how returns will be dealt with and whose responsibility it is to return items that are unwanted within the seven-day *cooling off period*.

Terms and conditions should also specify what a customer should do if they have a complaint.

If the online service does not have a standard set that can be adapted for your use then the services of a solicitor might be helpful. Alternatively, the distance selling hub provided by the Office of Fair Trading has helpful advice and documents to download and share with customers.

'All websites that are selling online must have a set of terms and conditions.'

Privacy and data protection

All business owners are legally required to ensure that any personal details customers pass on are stored in a secure manner and not shared with third parties except for the purposes of fulfilling orders. Personal details include names, addresses, email addresses, bank account information, credit card and debit card details. You can find out more about compliance with the Data Protection Act 1998 on the Information Commissioner's website.

Most online sellers won't be processing credit card or debit card payments themselves as these will be handled by a third party such as PayPal. However if you do then you will need to make sure that your processes for storing this information are PCI DSS compliant.

PCI DSS is a set of security standards that help reduce the risk of your customers' card data falling into the wrong hands. You can find out more information about compliance with the standards on the PCI Security Standards Council website.

'The Data Protection Act 1998 requires every business gathering personal data to register with the Information Commissioners Office unless they are exempt.'

Website cookies

Cookies are small pieces of code which are typically stored on the computer of a website user. They are used to store information such as user names and passwords so that people can log in quickly to sites like Face-book, Amazon or eBay.

They can also be used to track what visitors do on a website so that owners can understand how people use their site and improve it. When used like this they are anonymous and websites don't record any personal information.

In 2012, the UK Information Commissioner required that all websites make it clear to their users about how they use cookies stored on their website visitors' computers.

If websites don't comply with this requirement then they may be fined. Most online selling sites already comply with this requirement and sellers don't need to do anything. However, if you are running your own online shop then you may need to add information to your website. You can find out more about the requirements on the Information Commissioner's website.

Data protection registration

The Data Protection Act 1998 requires every business gathering personal data to register with the Information Commissioner's Office unless they are exempt. According the Information Commissioner 'Personal data means data which relates to a living individual who can be identified from those data or from those data and other information which is in the possession of, or is likely to come into the possession of, the data controller'. A data controller is someone (or organisation) responsible for receiving or handling personal data.

In other words this refers to any information you gather which identifies an individual person. This might be by name, address, email address or even photograph.

If you are only keeping information relating to accounts and marketing for your online selling then it is likely you will be exempt from registering with the Information Commissioner.

If you have your own hosted online shop and it is using software like Bigcommerce which is based outside the UK then there is some debate about whether you need to register. This is because you are sharing data overseas. You can call the Information Commissioner's Office for advice on 0303 123 1113.

If you are using personal information from people for any of the following:

- Accountancy/Auditing
- Administration of Justice and legal services
- Advertising, marketing and public relations for others
- Canvassing political support amongst the electorate
- Constituency casework
- Consultancy and advisory services
- Credit referencing
- Crime prevention and prosecution of offenders (including use of CCTV for their purposes)
- Debt administration and factoring

- Education

- Health administration and provision of health services

- Insurance administration

- Journalism and media

- Legal services

- Mortgage/insurance broking/insurance administration

- Pastoral care

- Pensions administration

- Personal information processed by or obtained from a credit reference agency

- Private investigation

- Provision of financial services and advice

- Property management (including the selling of property)

- Provision of childcare

- Research

- Trading and sharing in personal information

'If you have your own online shop you will also need to include a privacy statement.'

Then you will need to register your use of the data with the Information Commissioner. It costs £35 per year to register and you can do so online at http://ico.org.uk/

Privacy statement

If you have your own online shop you will also need to include a privacy statement. This explain how you store customers' personal information, what you do with it, how customers can find out what information you hold about them and the cookies that your website uses to track activity. If you are registered with the Information Commissioner then you can add a link to your own registration.

Summing Up

- Unless you are only selling items that are no longer wanted then any income earned by selling online will be taxable.

- You will need to register with the Inland Revenue for Self Assessment and complete an additional tax return form regardless of whether you are also employed.

- UK income tax is payable at the current rates on any income over and above the allowance you will have for the year.

- If your business earns over the current VAT threshold in a year then you will also need to register to pay VAT.

- Anyone earning over the current limit for self-employed earnings will also be required to pay an additional Class 2 National Insurance contribution.

- You can set up a basic bookkeeping system by storing information about your sales, your purchases and your bank statement.

- There is a variety of free and paid for software that you can use online to help you manage your accounts and make completing your Self Assessment tax return easier.

- Everyone selling online in the UK is required to comply with the distance selling regulations.

- Online buyers have a seven-day cooling off period to change their mind and return the goods to you. If a buyer chooses to use their cooling off period you must refund their money within 30 days.

- If you are running your own website you must include a set of terms and conditions and a privacy statement.

Appendix 1

Calculation Sheets

The next few pages contain a number of sheets that you can use to help calculate the cost of your products, postage, selling fees, materials, overheads and equipment.

All of these forms are also available to download and print out from my website www.womanontheedgeofreality.com. You can use the following link to find the documents easily: http://bit.ly/online-selling-book.

Pricing products calculation sheet

This form will help you work out the starting price of your product before selling it online.

Cost of materials (from the materials cost calculation form, page 115)	£
Cost of your time (from the time cost calculation form, page 116)	£
Cost of your overheads (from the overheads cost calculation form, page 114)	£
Cost of equipment (from the equipment cost calculation form, page 117)	£
Cost of listing fees	£
Cost of postage (if this is NOT added separately)	£
Total cost of item	**£**
This is the minimum amount that you need to charge for each item to cover all of your costs	

Calculating postage costs

Write here the cost of your packing materials (using the materials cost calculation form, page 115).	£
Write here the cost to send this item to your buyer. Use www.royalmail.com to calculate the cost of postage.	£
Write here the cost of parking at your post office.	£
Write here an amount of money for petrol to get to the post office.	£
Total cost of postage	£
This is the minimum amount that you need to charge for postage to a buyer when your item sells. You can include this in your product price if it is not added separately.	

Selling fees calculation sheet

This form will help you work out how much it will cost you to sell an item online.

Write here the listing fee for your item.	£
Write here the final valuation fee for your item.	£
Write here any extra costs for listing your item such as additional photographs.	£
Write here the amount you will be charged by your online payment processor for buyers paying by credit or debit card.	£
Total cost of fees	£
You will need to add this amount to your product pricing calculation.	

Calculating the cost of your overheads

This form will help you work out an amount of money that you can add into your product pricing to cover your overheads.

Overheads are things you need to run your business but aren't directly added to the cost of any particular item you might make or sell. This might include the cost of membership fees for some online sites or if you are hosting your own online shop.

Overheads		
Write the name and cost of anything you buy to run your business in the boxes below. Divide the cost by the number of items in each packet or box; this will give you an individual cost for a single item. For example, if a box of 100 padded envelopes costs £13 then dividing that by 100 means each one costs 13p.		
Item	**Total Cost**	**Single Item Cost**
	£	£
	£	£
	£	£
	£	£
	£	£
	£	£
	£	£
	£	£
	£	£
	£	£
	£	£
	£	£

Calculating the cost of materials

This form will help you work out the costs of the materials you use to make your products. You can then add this cost to your product pricing form.

Materials are those things that you actually make products from such as beads, wires, paper or card.

Materials
Write the name and cost of anything you buy to make your items in the boxes below. Divide the cost by the number of items you use in each item you make; this will give you an individual cost for a single item.
For example, if you buy a box of 1,000 beads costing £20 and you use 100 in each item you make the single item cost would be £2.

Material	Total Cost	Single Material Cost
	£	£
	£	£
	£	£
	£	£
	£	£
	£	£
	£	£
	£	£
	£	£
	£	£
	£	£
	£	£
	£	£

Calculating the cost of your time

Example

A. Write here how much you would like to earn from your online selling every year	£1,000
B. Write here how many hours you would like to work each week selling online.	5
C. Multiply line B by 52. This is how many hours you will work each year.	
Divide line A by line C. This is how much each hour of your time will be worth. Round up to the nearest penny.	

Your calculation

A. Write here how much you would like to earn from your online selling every year	£
B. Write here how many hours you would like to work each week on online selling	
C. Multiply line B by 52. This is how many hours you will work each year.	
Divide line A by line C. This is how much each hour of your time is worth. Round up to the nearest penny.	£

Calculating the cost of your equipment

You need to include an amount of money in the price of each item you sell which covers the cost of any equipment you might need to use. This might include cameras, printers or computers. You will need to use a separate form for each piece of equipment.

Example

A. Cost of equipment.	£500
B. Divide line A by 3. This gives you an annual cost for your equipment over three years.	£166.66
C. Divide line B by 52. This gives you a weekly cost for your equipment.	£3.21
D. Divide line C by the number of hours you plan to work on your business each week, you will find this on the calculating the cost of your time sheet. This gives you an hourly cost for the equipment.	£0.64
E. Divide line D by the number of items you make in an hour. This will tell you how much your equipment costs for a single item.	£0.064

A. Cost of equipment.	£
B. Divide line A by 3. This gives you an annual cost for your equipment over three years.	£
C. Divide line B by 52. This gives you a weekly cost for your equipment.	£
D. Divide line C by the number of hours you plan to work on your business each week, you will find this on the calculating the cost of your time sheet. This gives you an hourly cost for the equipment.	£
E. Divide line D by the number of items you make in an hour. This will tell you how much your equipment costs for a single item.	£

Appendix 2

Activity tick sheet for selling online

This tick sheet can also be downloaded from my website by typing in the following web address: http://bit.ly/online-selling-book

Task	Completed
Do you have a UK credit or debit card? You can't sell online without one.	
Do you have some items or services to sell?	
Have you decided on the best place to sell each item or service?	
Do you have a computer and a personal email address?	
Do you have a camera and a printer?	
Have you sourced your packing materials (if needed)?	
Have you worked out the selling price for each item or service?	
Have you worked out the fees you will pay to sell each item or service?	
Do you have good-quality photographs of items you are selling?	
Have your photographs been resized to reduce the file size?	
Have you created your product or service description?	
Have you decided on the correct category for your item or service?	
Have you identified a source for your stock of items to sell?	

Have you set up your online payment processing account?	
Have you worked out the cost of posting your items to buyers?	
Have you worked out your 4 Ps to help market each item or service?	
Have you registered with the HMRC for Self Assessment?	
Have your registered with the HMRC for VAT if necessary?	
Have you created policies to comply with the UK Distance Selling Regulations, Ecommerce Regulations and the Data Protection Act?	

Appendix 3

Useful sites

Marketplaces

Alibris – www.alibris.co.uk

Amazon – www.amazon.co.uk

Artfire – www.artfire.com

eBay – www.ebay.co.uk

Etsy – www.etsy.com

Play – www.playtrade.com

Auction sites

Avabid – www.avabid.com

CQout – www.cqout.com

eBay – www.ebay.co.uk

eBid – uk.ebid.net

Specialist Auctions – www.specialistauctions.com

Total bids – www.totalbids.co.uk

Print on demand/create on demand

Blurb – www.blurb.co.uk

Bookbaby – www.bookbaby.com

CafePress – www.cafepress.co.uk

CD Baby – www.cdbaby.com

Createspace – www.createspace.com

Kindle Direct – kdp.amazon.com

Lulu – www.lulu.com

MoPix – www.getmopix.com

Photobox – www.photobox.co.uk

Smashwords – www.smashwords.com

Spreadshirts – www.spreadshirt.co.uk

Streetshirts – www.streetshirts.co.uk

Zazzle – www.zazzle.co.uk

Fine art, images and photography

123rf – www.123rf.com

Art Gallery UK – http://www.artgallery.co.uk

Bigstock – www.bigstockphoto.com

Dreamstime – www.dreamstime.com

Shutterstock – www.shutterstock.com

Fotolia – www.fotolia.com

Fotosearch – www.fotosearch.com

iStockPhoto – www.istockphoto.com

Stockxchng – www.sxc.hu

Services

Craigslist – http://www.craigslist.org

Elance – www.elance.com

Freelancer – www.freelancer.co.uk

Fiverr – www.fiverr.com

Gumtree – www.gumtree.com

Instant shops

Big Commerce – www.bigcommerce.com

ECWID – www.ecwid.com

ekmPowershop – www.ekmpowershop.com

Instant Cart – www.instantcart.com

Shopify – www.shopify.com

Payment processors

Checkout with Amazon – http://payments.amazon.co.uk/business

Google Wallet – http://wallet.google.com

Moneybookers (Skrill) – www.moneybookers.com

Nochex – http://www.nochex.com

PayPal – https://www.paypal.com

Secure Pay – www.securepay.com

WorldPay – http://www.worldpay.com

Email mailing list systems

Aweber – www.aweber.com

Get Response – www.getresponse.co.uk

iContact – www.icontact.com

MailChimp – www.mailchimp.com

Domain name registration

123 Reg – www.123-reg.co.uk

Easily – www.easily.co.uk

Names – www.names.co.uk

UK Reg – www.ukreg.com

Telephone number providers

SwitchboardFREE – www.switchboardfree.co.uk

TelWise – www.telwise.co.uk

QR code creators

bitly – www.bitly.com

QR Pro – www.qrpro.co.uk

Quick QR – www.quikqr.com

Glossary

Add to cart

This is the link in an online shop that allows buyers to add items to a virtual shopping cart before they go to the checkout.#

Affiliate Marketing

A marketing method used by a company to sell its products by enlisting individuals or companies (affiliates) to promote its products/services for a commission.

Back-up

A back-up is a copy of all the information contained on a computer that is stored somewhere else.

Bumping up

Is where adverts on Gumtree can be pushed to the top of the listings shown to users by payment of a small amount of money.

Cooling off period

A seven-day period where online buyers can change their mind and return the goods for a full refund.

Cost price

The cost price is the cost to make a product without any profit being added.

Drop Shipping

A process where a customer orders a product and someone else supplies it directly to them on behalf of the seller.

Ecommerce

Ecommerce is the selling of products online including taking orders and accepting payments.

Final valuation fee

The final valuation fee is the charge made by online sellers like eBay when an item sells. The amount charged is usually based on the item's final sale price and category.

Gross profit

The gross profit is the difference between the amount charged to buyers and the cost of making a product or providing a service, before deducting overheads and tax.

Hosting space

Hosting space is the space provided by a commercial company on a computer attached to the Internet allowing someone to store the programme files that run their website.

ISBN number

This is the unique number that specifies a particular book in global databases

Listings

These are a list of directory entries of items for sale shown on an online shopping site.

Merchant services

Refer to the provision of payment processing services by a third party company such as PayPal. They allow online sellers to process buyer's payments by credit or debit card.

Overheads

These are the on-going expenses related to running a business such as monthly subscription charges not included in the cost of making products, buying stock or providing services.

Payment processing charge

This is the charge made by online payment processors for each buyer transaction which is paid by credit or debit card.

Print on demand/on-demand

Products created only when they are ordered. The service provides for postage to the customer as well.

Profit margin

Is the amount by which sales in a business exceed the costs of the business.

Royalty free

This refers to the right to use copyrighted material without the need to pay for each individual use. It usually involves a single payment which allows the purchaser to use the image or photograph they have bought for a set number of times.

Royalty payment

Is a payment made to a writer, musician or film--maker that is the difference between the amount charged for their book by a print on demand publisher and the costs to produce and post each item.

Self Assessment

Is the system used by the HMRC that allows taxpayers to assess their own tax liabilities.

Selling price

This is the price an item is actually sold for in an online shop, marketplace or auction.

Shipping charge

The total cost of posting items to a buyer including packing materials and driving to the post office.

Standard product numbering systems

Refers to the system by which individual items are given a number that identifies them in an online shop. This includes ISBN numbers for books.

Stock

Are the items that someone buys in or makes in order to sell for a profit.

Upsell

Refers to a marketing technique that encourages people to increase their orders by purchasing related items. For example encouraging someone to buy chips to go with the fish they have ordered.

User verification fee

This is a fee charged by some online shops and payment processors that proves the person opening an account is a real person. It involves the payment of or debit from a UK based credit card, debit card or bank account.

Need2Know

Variable overhead cost

These are the business expenses which fluctuate on a monthly basis. They might include the cost of office supplies, packaging, listing fees or telephone calls. They are the opposite of fixed overhead costs such as monthly subscription fees.

Help List

Amazon UK

www.amazon.co.uk/gp/help/customer/display.html
Amazon.co.uk (Customer Services), Patriot Court, 1-9 The Grovetown, Slough, Berkshire SL1 1QP
Tel: 0800 496 1081
The Amazon help pages are full of information about everything an online seller needs to know about using their services. Includes selling on the marketplace, Kindle store and Amazon associates. Sellers can place a telephone call to eBay when they are logged in to the website.

Business Link Helpline

Tel: 0845 600 9006 (Monday to Friday, 9am to 6pm)
The helpline provides a quick response service if you have simple questions about starting or running a business. It also provides a more in--depth service if you have more complex enquiries.

British Chambers of Commerce

www.britishchambers.org.uk
65 Petty France, London, SW1H 9EU
Tel: 020 7654 5800
The British Chambers of Commerce is an independent business network of local chambers of commerce which supports business of all sizes. You can locate the contact details for your local chamber as well as helpful business advice and information.

Clear Books

www.clearbooks.co.uk/
Clear Books Limited, Masters House, 107 Hammersmith Road, West Kensington, London, W14 0QH.
Tel: 08448 160 616
Clear Books Limited provide an online system to manage business accounts.

Companies House

www.companieshouse.gov.uk
Companies House, Crown Way, Cardiff, CF14 3UZ
Tel: 0303 1234 500
Companies House provides services that incorporate and dissolve limited companies. It stores company information required by the Companies Act and makes it available to the public.

eBay UK

http://pages.ebay.co.uk/help/index.html
EBAY (UK) LIMITED, 9TH FLOOR, 107 CHEAPSIDE, LONDON, EC2V 6DN
Tel: 0844 656 3747 (Customer Service)
eBay help pages are full of information about everything an online seller needs to know about using eBay. Including selling formats, taking payments, creating listings and how to deal with disputes.
Sellers can place a telephone call to eBay when they are logged in to the website.

Freeagent.com

www.freeagent.com
40 Torphichen Street, Edinburgh, EH3 8JB, United Kingdom
Tel: 0131 447 0011
Freeagent.com is one of the UK's largest online accounting services.

Google

www.google.co.uk
adwords.google.com
analytics.google.com Google UK Ltd, 123 Buckingham Palace Road, London, SW1W 9SH
Tel: 020 7031 3000
Google is the most popular search engine in the world and it provides many different services for small and large businesses. The most important of the services allow you to track website visitors (Analytics) and place adverts on to the search engine (Adwords).

Gov.UK

www.gov.uk
A national website run by the UK government providing a wide range of advice to UK residents including information about business and tax.
HM Revenue and Customs (HMRC)
HM Revenue & Customs, Self Assessment, PO Box 4000, Cardiff CF14 8HR.
Tel: 0845 900 0444 (self assessment helpline)
Tel: 0845 010 9000 (VAT helpline)

www.hmrc.gov.uk

Self Assessment Helpline: 0300 200 3310
The HMRC website is full of useful information to help individuals and businesses sort out their tax liabilities and responsibilities. You can register online for Self Assessment and VAT.

ICO – Information Commissioner

www.ico.org.uk
Information Commissioner's Office, Wycliffe House, Water Lane, Wilmslow, Cheshire, SK9 5AF
Tel: 0303 123 1113 (helpline)
Textphone: 01625 545860
The Information Commissioner's office is responsible for compliance with the UK Data Protection Act and Privacy in the UK.

National Enterprise Network

www.nationalenterprisenetwork.org
12 Stephenson Court, Fraser Road, Priory Business Park, Bedford, MK44 3WJ
Tel: 01234 831623
The National Enterprise Network offers impartial and independent advice on starting or developing a small business in England. They provide a directory of regional agencies to contact.

Nielsen Book Data

www.nielsenbookdata.co.uk

Nielsen Book Data (Head Office), 3rd Floor, Midas House, 62 Goldsworth Road, Woking, Surrey, GU21 6LQ

Tel: 01483 712 200

Nielsen allocates ISBN numbers to publishers, advises publishers on the correct way to implement the ISBN system and maintains a database of publishers for book sellers.

Office of Fair Trading – Distance Selling Hub

dshub.tradingstandards.gov.uk

The Distance Selling hub is provided by the Office of Fair Trading to give guidance to retailers and business support organisations about the legal requirements that that affect buying and selling goods and services via the internet, phone, mail order, email, interactive TV or text.

PCI Security Standards Council

www.pcisecuritystandards.org

PCI Security Standards Council LLC, 401 Edgewater Place, Suite 600, Wakefield, MA, USA 01880.

Tel: +1-781-876-8855

The PCI Security Standards Council is responsible for the development, enhancement, storage, dissemination and implementation of security standards for account data protection.

Princes Trust

www.princes-trust.org.uk

The Prince's Trust, Prince's Trust House, 9 Eldon Street, London, EC2M 7LS.

Tel: 020 7543 1234

Minicom: 0207 543 1374

The Prince's Trust Enterprise programme helps young people between the ages of 18 and 30 who are interested in self-employment to explore and test their ideas, write plans and start their own businesses

Prowess 2.0 Women in Business

www.prowess.org.uk

39 Merton Road, Norwich NR2 3TT, UK

The Prowess website provides information, resources and directories of local, women-friendly business support and networks.

Quick File

www.quickfile.co.uk

219 Kensington High Street, Kensington, London, W8 6BD.

Quick File is a free online accounting service for small to medium-sized businesses. It allows users to create professional-looking invoices, track what's owed to you and by you.

Seed Network

www.seednetwork.com

Seed, PO Box 1487, Oxford, OX4 9DR

The seed network is an online community for women who are building their own businesses. It provides information, education, training, support and online networking along the principles of sustainable co--operation and mutual empowerment.

Start Up Donut (The)

www.startupdonut.co.uk

BHP Information Solutions, 4th Floor, Albert House, 111 Victoria Street, Bristol, BS1 6AX

Tel: 0117 904 2224

The Start Up Donut website provides information and resources for business owners about marketing, law, IT and tax. Registration on the website is free of charge and allows users to access local sites where available.

startups.co.uk

www.startups.co.uk

Crimson Publishing Ltd, Westminster House, Kew Road, Richmond, Surrey, TW9 2ND

Tel: 020 8334 1647

Startups UK is a website that contains lots of useful information, advice and guidance about starting a business in the UK. There is a free to join online forum where you can chat with others in business and ask questions.

The Wholesale Forums UK

www.thewholesaleforums.co.uk
Wholesale Forums is UK-based community forum for trade buyers and suppliers. It is free to join and ask questions. They also have a specialist forum for eBay, Amazon and other online marketplaces.

VentureNavigator

www.venturenavigator.co.uk
VentureNavigator is a free online business support service offering business information resources and business assessments. It also provides an online community of entrepreneurs who share startup advice.

Viking

www.viking-direct.co.uk
Office Depot International (UK) Ltd, 501 Beaumont Leys Lane, Leicester, LE4 2BN
Tel: 0844 412 3435
Viking are wholesale suppliers of stationery items in the UK. They provide a next-day delivery on most items.

Woman on the Edge of Reality

www.womanontheedgeofreality.com
2 Princes Court, Puddletown, Dorchester, Dorset, DT2 8UE
Tel: 0843 289 2142
The Woman on the Edge of Reality blog contains a large amount of information for authors who want to market their books as well as suggestions about how to use social media effectively. Downloads of the forms contained in the Appendices are also available from the page about this book.

Women in Business Network

www.wibn.co.uk

WIBN, The Grange, East End, Furneux Pelham, Nr Buntingford, Herts, SG9 OJT

The Women in Business Network (WIBN) is a membership organisation for women who meet monthly. Members are encouraged to support each other through collaboration and the sharing of business contacts and opportunities. The WIBN website has a directory of groups across the UK.

Book List

500 Social Media Marketing Tips: Essential Advice, <u>Hints and Strategy for Business</u>, Andrew Macarthy.

Facebook Business Basics: The Jargon-Free Guide to Simple Facebook Success, Lewis Love.

How to Make Money Using Etsy: A Guide to the Online Marketplace for Crafts and Handmade Products, Timothy Adam.

How to Twitter for Business Success: Everything Business Owners Need to Know About Twitter Made Easy! Nicky Kriel.

LinkedIn Made Easy: Business Social Networking Simplified, Linda Parkinson--Hardman

Selling on Amazon: How You Can Make A Full-Time Income Selling on Amazon, Brian Patrick.

The eBay Business Handbook: How anyone can build a business and make big money on eBay.co.uk, Robert Pugh

The Ultimate Guide to Marketing Your Business With Pinterest, Gabriela Taylor.

References

Amazon Kindle Direct Publishing Help Files. Source: Amazon.co.uk, accessed 29th May 2013.

Bazaar Voice Conversation Index. Source: Bazaar Voice, page 25, accessed 10th April 2013.

Cookies. Source: Information Commissioner's Office, accessed 30th May 2013.

Crown Copyright: Consumer Credit Act 1974. Source: Legislation.Gov.UK.

Crown Copyright: Data Protection Act 1998. Source: Legislation.Gov.UK.

Do Online Reviews Affect Product Sales? The Role of Reviewer Characteristics and Temporal Effects. Source: Social Science Research Network, 7th January 2008.

eBay Company Overview. Source eBay.co.uk, accessed 29th May 2013.

eBay Help Pages. Source: eBay.co.uk, accessed 29th May 2013

Crown Copyright: The Electronic Commerce (EC Directive) Regulations 2002. Source: Legislation.Gov.UK.

Etsy Statistics. Source: Etsy.co.uk, accessed 30th May 2013.

Four self-published authors on New York Times e-book bestseller list: Source The Guardian, 2nd August 2012.

GS1 UK and Amazon Sellers. Source: GS1 UK, accessed 29th May 2013.

Google Grabs More Market Share. Source: Search Engine Watch, 15th March 2013

Crown Copyright: Internet Access Quarterly Update Bulletin, Q3, 2012. Source: Office for National Statistics

Crown Copyright: Sale of Goods Act 1979. Source: Legislation.Gov.UK.

Self-published e-book author becomes Amazon's top seller: Source The Guardian, 8th February 2012

Selling At Amazon.co.uk Marketplace: Source Amazon.co.uk, accessed 29th May 2013

The UK's Ecommerce Regulations. Source: Outlaw.com.

The UK's Distance Selling Regulations: Source Outlaw.com.

Top Ten Alternatives To eBay. Source: Top Ten Reviews, accessed 30th May 2013.

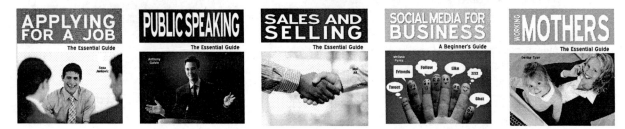